From Notepad to iPad

From Notepad to iPad

Using Apps and Web Tools to Engage a New Generation of Students

Matthew D. Gillispie

Routledge
Taylor & Francis Group

NEW YORK AND LONDON

First published 2014
by Routledge
711 Third Avenue, New York, NY 10017

and by Routledge
2 Park Square, Milton Park, Abingdon, Oxon OX14 4RN

Routledge is an imprint of the Taylor & Francis Group, an informa business

Library of Congress Cataloging-in-Publication Data
Gillispie, Matthew.
  From notepad to iPad: using apps and Web tools to engage a new
  generation of students/Matthew Gillispie.
  pages cm
  Includes bibliographical references.
  1. Computer—assisted instruction.   2. Application software.
  3. iPad (Computer).   4. Tablet computers.   I. Title.
  LB1028.5.G538 2013
  371.33'4—dc23
  2013034346

ISBN: 978-0-415-73533-9 (hbk)
ISBN: 978-0-415-73206-2 (pbk)
ISBN: 978-1-315-81926-6 (ebk)

Typeset in Bembo and Helvetica Neue
by Florence Production Ltd, Stoodleigh, Devon, UK

Printed and bound in the United States of America by Publishers Graphics,
LLC on sustainably sourced paper.

To Ashlin, Kelli, and innovative teachers everywhere

Contents

About the Author

Matt Gillispie is in his sixth year of teaching English and Speech for Lancaster City Schools. He graduated from Kent State University in 2008 with a bachelor's in Integrated Language Arts. He received his master's in the Art of Teaching in 2012 from Marygrove College. He was co-awarded a $100,000 grant in 2011 for his students to use iPads in the classroom and has been featured in Ohio Department of Education's Teacher Showcase Series focusing on project-based learning with iPads. He speaks to other teachers about using technology at conferences. He currently resides in Grove City, Ohio.

Acknowledgments

Many people are responsible for the creation of this book. First and foremost, everything my students and I have learned with regard to technology would not be possible if not for eTech Ohio. They offered not only us, but 15 other schools, the chance to put technology in the hands of our students by awarding us a grant. I never would have been able to change my teaching and engage my students if not for this wonderful organization. Thank you, eTech Ohio.

I also want to acknowledge my principal, Jack Greathouse, Dean Scott Matchett, and our district's Technology Director, Kevin Snyder. It was enough for eTech to award this grant, but implementing iPads would not have been as rewarding and successful if not for a trusting administration. The three of them trusted our grant team to use the technology the way we knew it could be used, and they put no limits on what my students could do with iPads.

I also want thank Tracy Cindric, the technology coach assigned to our district by eTech Ohio. She was such a wonderful resource and always came to our school with new apps to share, ideas, and tutorials covering how to use these tools. As lessons floundered and apps failed to serve their purpose, she encouraged me not to give up on this transformation of my classroom. I am extremely grateful to her.

I also want to give a big thank you to Bob Sickles for giving me the opportunity to voice my successes and struggles with the iPad in this book. I am extremely grateful to you for making my dream of becoming an author come true. Thank you for your guidance and for believing in this project.

Finally, I need to mention the two other teachers who worked exhaustively with me throughout this transformation of our classrooms: Ashlin Henderson and Kelli Marvin. We worked together through this process of transforming our classrooms. Some of the tools and activities highlighted in this book involved a collaborative effort; while I am providing a narrative of how I implemented them in my classroom, I never would have known about some of them had these two colleagues not introduced them to me. We discussed problems that arose, assessment strategies, and so much more. I am definitely a better teacher having worked with them.

Introduction

I currently do not own a cell phone. Ironic, right? Here I am, typing a book for current and aspiring teachers about using apps and web tools in the classroom, and I do not own a cell phone. The technology I use in my private life is quite modest. I own a home computer, a laptop. It's a cheap one too. I bought it six years ago, and I am proud to say that it is still working.

You will not see me at home using a phone or iPad and watching television, all the while holding conversations with others at the dinner table as I try to eat my dinner. That's probably a good thing, as I could not perform all these activities at once. Although, I am amazed by my nieces and other youngsters who are able to multitask like crazy.

The truth is that I choose to live a simpler life. I do not own a cell phone because I have found that they are keeping people from really communicating with one another. One of my biggest pet peeves is holding live conversations with people who can't stop interacting with their phones. This can be infuriating, especially when dining with others. Unfortunately, this behavior is becoming a norm in our society. I can't tell you how many times I have been in a social situation and a friend or family member, unaware of their rudeness, is texting away while I am frantically trying to keep their interest.

While I choose not to let technology dominate my life, I will admit that I know how to use different types and brands of technology. I am constantly fascinated by what technology can do, how it can make our lives easier, and how efficient it can be. I just know that if I were to have some mobile device with me at all times, I would quickly develop the habits that infuriate me.

This cautious approach to technology carries over into my classroom. Each year, I try to find informational texts about the importance of technology and how technology such as the iPad or iPhone has positively and negatively affected our society. These texts not only help teach informational text standards, but they also provide students with reasons why they need to learn technology, how to appropriately use it, and which tools they can use to make their lives easier.

With this instruction in mind, you should know that my classroom is a completely different atmosphere from my home. Despite my lack of personal mobile devices, I have, throughout the course of two school years, become familiar with how to use, implement, and manage technology in my classroom.

As a result, my classroom is more innovative than one might expect from a person who does not own a cell phone.

Technology is all around my students in Room 167 at Lancaster High School. Let me give you a clear picture: I have a desktop computer, a MimioBoard, a laptop, a MacBook, a school-issued iPad, and 30 iPads, each of which is assigned to students at the beginning of the year to use for the 42 minutes we spend together each day.

My students use them daily; they grab them out of the cart when they first enter the classroom and put them back at the end of class when the bell rings. This is all due to a wonderful organization: eTech Ohio. They are the reason why my students and I were afforded an opportunity to use 30 iPads in the classroom on a regular basis. In the spring of 2011, I, along with three other teachers, applied for a grant titled Transforming Teaching and Learning. Offered by eTech Ohio, over 100 schools were eligible to apply, and we ended up being one of the 16 schools that were awarded this grant.

As we wrote this grant, our grant team and I worked long hours to write a document that illustrated our need for mobile devices. The school district in which we work, Lancaster, is a hodgepodge of economic groups; as a teacher, I can see the digital divide in each of the six classes I teach every day. In a country where there are fewer factory jobs and more careers that require proficiency with technology, we applied for this grant with the intention of creating an equal playing field for all students in our classrooms. My philosophy is that all students should have a chance at a successful future when they graduate from high school and move on to the "real world." The eTech organization understands this divide, and they afforded us an opportunity to help meet the needs of all of our students.

This brings me to the purpose of this book. After two years of transforming the way I teach, my classroom is a completely different environment from what it used to be when I stepped into the classroom five years ago. I have provided my successes and my failures. They are described in great detail. Nothing is off limits.

I want to stress that this is simply what I have done in my classroom; by no means is it the correct and only way to use technology in the classroom. I had some help through professional development, my colleagues involved in the grant, and my own research. However, I found early on in the process exactly how innovative and new this technology is to education. It will only become more popular, and teachers need more resources to help them implement this technology efficiently and correctly. The Internet is a start; it is a great place to find new tools to use. However, after a bit of time perusing the Web, I have found that many sites only offer tools. They do not offer sample lessons, management strategies, and activities. Teachers who have experience with this technology in their classrooms are the best source to understand exactly how these apps and tools work when integrated into lessons.

I assure you that the dramatic change in my instruction did not occur overnight. In fact, I can think of 10 different instances in the first six months of this process in which I wanted to chuck the technology out the window, forget it ever existed, and revert back to my old methods of instruction. In many ways, this experience with technology reminds me of my first year of teaching; for the first five months with the iPads, I felt as if I had no idea what I was doing. Many lessons floundered during the formative months of the transformation of teaching, as an app failed to serve its purpose or was not as reliable as I initially thought.

Technology does indeed have its flaws, some of which will be highlighted in this book. On the other hand, with patience and proper use, it can also create a classroom of students more engaged than you ever thought was possible. The following chapters provide a narrative of how I achieved this and my path to a true 21st-century classroom.

The landscape of the job market is rapidly changing, and our classrooms need to adapt. Changing from the 20th-century to the 21st-century classroom has been an arduous task. But I forget about this when a student tells me he or she has never enjoyed school or English until he or she stepped into my classroom. This comment is one of the most rewarding remarks I have heard, and it tells me that my hard work was worth it. After just a short time of using iPads, I assure you, as a former traditional, drill-and-practice teacher, I will never go back to the way I used to teach. I assure you, if I, somebody who refuses to let technology dominate his personal life, can make this dramatic change with my approach to teaching, you can too. Hopefully, this book will give you some tool, whether it is a classroom management technique website or an app, that will help you as you make this gargantuan leap to a new and exciting era of teaching and learning.

Where to Start and How to Plan Lessons

I studied to become a teacher during a period of transition in education. When I graduated high school, SMART Boards were not in the classroom, and I did not know what they were or what they could do. As I completed my undergraduate degree at Kent State University and completed field observations, I then saw many of them pop up in school districts. Then, when I student taught, SMART Boards and other interactive whiteboards became the norm in many classrooms, as I rarely entered a building that did not have one. In a period of four years of leaving high school as a student and re-entering it as a student teacher, the landscape of technology in the classroom saw a great change.

It was also during this time that I was first introduced to the *future* of technology in the classroom setting. Before and during my student teaching, many professors emphasized the importance of using Web tools in the classroom to teach reading and writing. Thus, professors introduced me to wikis, blogging, podcasting, Movie Maker, and other interactive websites known as Web 2.0 tools. Most importantly, these courses stressed that these tools should be used by students, not just teachers.

The Dilemma Facing Schools Today

Even though I was introduced to some of the tools available in 2007, implementing them in the classroom was a completely different story. While student teaching in what many would consider an affluent district, the only tech tool available for daily use was a SMART Board, which I would not exactly call student-centered technology. Yes, I was also able to check out time in a computer lab or bring a cart of laptops to the classroom. However, with about 50 teachers in the school, it was nearly impossible to reserve time to use any of these resources, as they were usually booked months in advance by other teachers.

My students and I had even less technology available my first year of teaching. My school had a computer lab, but with a staff of well over 100 teachers, my time in it was scarce. The only technology available to me within my own classroom was an overhead projector and a desktop computer. It was not exactly the environment my professors had prepared me for.

I knew I had to put student use of technology on the backburner for the time being; there was no way for my students and me to use Web tools when I could not even project my computer screen or sign up for lab time. Besides, the primary goal of any first-year teacher was to survive each day and try not to cry on the way home from work.

But then, over the course of three years, it seemed as if technology exploded at Lancaster High School. By the end of my first year, we received computer projectors and MimioBoards. I spent the next few years figuring out how to use an interactive whiteboard in my lessons. I would stand up in the front of my classroom each day testing out the newest website or tool I found the night before.

While I knew that using the technology was an added touch to the classroom experience, I quickly noticed that my students were *watching* me use technology. While our administrators would emphasize having students use the technology, having students come up to the interactive whiteboard one by one to use it quickly ate up a lot of class time. Thus, many of my lessons centered on students watching me use the technology to teach course content. I quickly became frustrated. I wanted this use of technology to be much more student-centered.

This highlights a dilemma in education: there is not enough technology available for students to use. If some districts are lucky, they can afford a computer lab for teachers to take their students to type up papers or create presentations. It is a startling notion that in the classroom, students are using programs such as Microsoft PowerPoint and Word, programs that have been around for well more than a decade, when their own cell phones have apps and other tools that can create a more engaging and innovative learning environment than the one education currently affords them.

I want to make clear that I do not have any prejudice against Microsoft; in fact, I incorporate its programs in my lessons quite frequently. However, when students leave the high-school setting, they will be expected to use other technological tools and programs besides Microsoft's Office. With the current state of technology in schools that focus on teacher-centered use of technology, we are not fostering an environment that focuses on college and career readiness. This is especially daunting because it is exactly what the Common Core Standards emphasize for students. While we do what we can to teach our content area, to be considered college- and career-ready, students need more of a well-rounded education. This must include proficiency with technology. Unfortunately, many schools fail to do this today because of a lack of money. If students are lucky, they can leave high school with a basic knowledge of Microsoft programs. In short, the current state of technology in education is not benefiting students.

I make this claim because it happened to me. My own lack of experience with technology created a rude awakening when I entered college for my undergraduate coursework. Before I had set foot in Kent State University, I only used three main tools in high school: the Internet, Microsoft Word, and Microsoft PowerPoint. By the end of my first two years of study at Kent State, I was expected to use Macs for video and photography classes. I was also expected to bring in my own digital camera for a photography course. I struggled at first; it took me a while to figure out how to simply cut, copy, and paste on a Mac computer. While my professors in these classes helped me at times, they had 30 other students in the course to tend to as well. For the most part, I was on my own.

At the time, I hated these classes, and I swore off Macs for the rest of my life. I did not understand why I, a future *English* teacher, would ever need to know how to edit videos or manipulate a photograph. But now, I can see that these classes instilled a valuable skill that I have used ever since: the ability to teach myself new and challenging programs. *This* is why I quickly became an advocate of technology in my classroom. This experience forced me to teach myself and take more ownership in my learning. Now that I can reflect on the experience, I do not want my students to have the same rude awakening I had when I entered college. The best way to do so would be to get technology in my students' hands and have them use it on a daily basis.

Unfortunately, as much as the teachers and administrators in my school knew the importance of technology, we had to make do with what we had. Before the iPads, I only had a desktop computer and an interactive whiteboard. I love the MimioBoard and still use it occasionally. But this tool alone does not put technology in the hands of students.

As a result, I would try to incorporate lessons in which students would come up to our one interactive whiteboard and move elements around. However, I was hungry for more. Simply demonstrating proficiency with the MimioBoard was not exactly going to prepare my students for their careers as doctors, lawyers, auto mechanics, nurses, etc. Moreover, having even five students get out of their seats one at a time to come up to the board, manipulate it, and then sit down wasted too much class time.

If you think about it, our job as teachers is more difficult today than ever. Not only must we teach our content, but because technology is advancing so quickly, we also have a duty to prepare our students for a future that we can't even imagine. Thus, we must teach content and skills beyond our specific content areas and foster other skills that will help students adapt and thrive to change.

21st Century Learning

To help give an overview of the skills students need, the Partnership for 21st Century Skills (2011) has developed the Framework for 21st Century Learning (Figure 1.1). It outlines the skills, knowledge, and experience students need to become competitive in a global economy. Overall, the diagram describes the skills students must master to be better prepared when they graduate and try to succeed in the job market. These include core subjects and content knowledge, learning and innovation skills, information, media and technology skills, and life and career skills.

Schools can prepare students for these skills by creating support systems that guide the teaching of these skills. These support systems are learning environ-

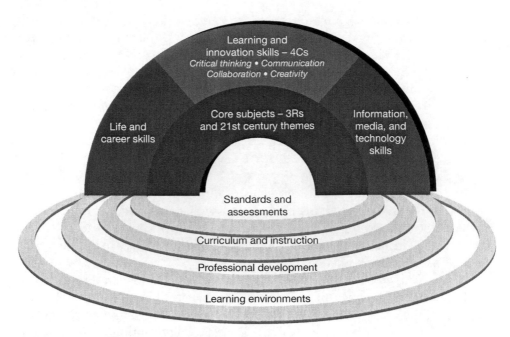

FIGURE 1.1 Framework for 21st Century Learning

ments, professional development, curriculum and instruction, and standards/ assessments. Thus, if we can transform these support systems to support 21st-century outcomes, students will be more prepared for a global economy.

The Partnership for 21st Century Skills (2011) addresses that "within the context of core knowledge instruction, students must learn the essential skills for success in today's world, such as critical thinking, [creativity], communication and collaboration." Thus, I address the framework by teaching my content with activities and lessons focused on giving students the learning and innovation skills they need. This area is known as the "4 Cs" (Partnership for 21st Century Skills, 2011). These skills, communication, collaboration, critical thinking, and creativity, are vital for students to have when they leave the K–12 setting and venture out into college and/or the workforce. Thus, they need to be explored further.

Critical Thinking

Critical thinking is, without a doubt, one of the most difficult skills to instill in students. I was quite shocked at how much the English/Language Arts classroom had changed when I re-entered high school as a student teacher. When I left high school and went to Kent State University to study for my undergrad, the standardized testing was becoming the norm; five years later, when I began teaching, I found that many teachers responded to it by teaching to the test (myself included). While I do feel that standardized tests hold value and validity, authentic assessment is far more valuable for students. This is especially true if we want to make them college- and career-ready. Students need an emotional connection to what they are learning; they want to know why they are learning concepts and how it pertains to their future. Authentic assessment can do this in ways selecting A, B, C, or D on a test will never be able to do.

The only critical thinking skills that testing really fosters is how to take a test, which is not the only skill students need to master. If you look at many of the questions on these tests, they truly do not match the complexity of questioning highlighted in Bloom's Taxonomy. Take, for example, the following question, regularly asked on standardized tests:

Which sentence summarizes the poem?

Looking at this question, the problem of standardized testing is highlighted; most of the questions ask students to simply comprehend a text or to identify a choice that clearly demonstrates that standard. Outside of basic comprehension and using the process of elimination, there is no critical thinking needed to answer this question correctly. A student simply needs to know how to summarize. Whenever I give my students reading assignments for homework, my expectation is that they will walk in the next day having read the selection and already able to summarize it. I will devote the first few minutes to answering questions to anything that is unclear. This way, we can delve into more rigorous concepts and activities. Today's standardized tests gage whether or not students have a basic comprehension of what they have read. This is not exactly going to make them college- and career-ready.

In addition, summarizing is a skill students learn in the primary grade levels. Yet, this is a question asked on a test students take to graduate from high school. Clearly, the higher levels of Bloom's Taxonomy can be addressed in more creative ways than a multiple-choice test allows.

To foster critical thinking, I use the higher levels of Bloom's Taxonomy. In my classroom, we use the synthesis level of Bloom's Taxonomy on a regular basis; we use technology to compose, modify, adapt, create, collaborate, structure, reinforce, evaluate, design, and plan. I do this because we need students to be thinkers and creators, not test-takers. Critical thinking helps students obtain the skills to think outside the box and create original products. Technology such as the iPad in the hands of students simply allows for more opportunities to use critical thinking skills. This is because many of the apps, when used correctly, force students to compose, modify, adapt, create, collaborate, structure, synthesize, reinforce, design, and plan in ways not possible in the classroom even 10 years ago. As a result, students are thinking about course content in a new manner that forces them to analyze it with true authentic assessments.

Communication

As an English and public speaking teacher, part of my job is to teach students communication skills. In the past, I have attempted to do so through the use of formal speaking situations and speeches. Students are supposed to give informative and persuasive presentations. However, I fail to regularly teach this important skill mainly due to the fact that it is not assessed on standardized tests. Moreover, having over 25 students give a three- to five-minute speech can eat up a lot of precious class time. Thus, this is a standard that I do not teach as much as I should.

With the implementation of the Common Core Standards, it is important to address speaking and listening skills. With the iPad, I have found quite a few ways to get students to practice public speaking. Many websites and apps, such as Padlet and Schoology, allow students to answer questions by opening up the iPad's Camera Roll to shoot a video response. I can also create exit slips in which students open up their e-mail and shoot/insert short videos to me through the iPad's e-mail feature. These tools not only allow for varied lessons and assessments, but for students to practice articulating themselves and their thoughts.

While speaking and listening skills are important, the iPad has provided more experiences for students to communicate their thoughts through the written word. Our standards teach primarily formal methods of communication and to do so through speeches and writing essays. However, with forums, texting, Twitter, social networking, and e-mail, there are many other ways to communicate in a classroom environment. These tools can create teachable moments to discuss when it is not appropriate to use slang and occasions in which it is permissible to not capitalize the letter I.

By implementing these new forms of communication in the classroom, I have seen an improvement in my students' quality of writing. Before the technology arrived, I constantly commiserated with my colleagues that text lingo would constantly pop up in formal essays. The iPad has created experiences in which I can create formal and informal writing opportunities in an online environment. As a result, they have a deeper understanding of what formal communication actually is, why it is important, and how and when to write in a formal manner. It is no coincidence that my students' use of text lingo in formal essays has dramatically decreased since the iPads arrived, as the device has created an opportunity to teach this skill in the classroom.

Students understand informal communication fairly well; they have their own dialect. We need to embrace this new dialect and incorporate it into our teaching; this way, we can teach students formal and informal language and when its use is appropriate and inappropriate. Social networking sites such as Twitter and Facebook (although I prefer Schoology, an educational version of Facebook), tools students use every single day, can be used in the classroom to teach students these vital communication skills that they will need later on in life.

I have learned this year that students can be extremely uncomfortable with online communication in the classroom. As we worked on a project-based learning assignment this year, I was amazed that so many students avoided apps and tools that promoted online communication and discussions. They preferred to meet with their groups face-to-face and many groups could not make decisions in an online environment. They needed to meet in person to get work done.

I have also found through the experience with the iPads that many students also do not know e-mail etiquette and sent e-mails with numerous spelling errors. Too many students did not know how to send an e-mail to more than one contact. They had never ever heard of "Ccing" an e-mail and what it means. These are skills that students need to be college- and career-ready, yet *teachers* are primarily using e-mail in the classroom to collaborate with one another. Thus, these are skills that we, teachers of any grade level and content area, need to teach whether we are adverse to technology or embrace it.

Collaboration

One of the skills that many employers are looking for in job candidates is people who are willing to work in a team. The old saying is correct: two heads are better than one. I try to instill this in my students by having them work in groups at least once a week; sometimes I select the groups, and sometimes I let them select their groups.

When they collaborate with one another, they are able to create products that can be better than what they would create on their own, as they bounce ideas off one another. It can provide confidence-boosting experiences and prepare them for the workforce. In addition, students need experiences in which they will work with people with differing opinions. I usually tell my students that they can communicate in their group without even looking at one another. I state that they can communicate in an online environment through social networking and may only meet a couple times throughout the course of the project. I then give them the tools, many of which will be highlighted in later chapters. While this does not win every student over, it does give them the coping skills needed to complete the project. I then relate my experiences in school when I had to work with people I did not exactly like.

Yes, some students take advantage of groups and slack while others take on far more than their share of the work. But this is a life skill that students need. This is why, for large projects, students have the opportunity to fire people from their groups. If someone is not performing or is not reliable, students have the chance to first warn that student by holding a group meeting, and then, if nothing has changed, fire that student. The terminated student then works by him or herself on that assignment or receives an alternative assignment. It is a great way to teach students real-life skills; if they are frequently undependable, consequences follow.

Creativity/Innovation

Working with the iPads this past year, I noticed more than ever how uncomfortable students were with 21st-century learning and technology. I realized it when I first announced we would use iPads in English class. A few students came up to me intimidated by the technology; they feared they would fail my class because they did not have any technology at home. Some even wanted to drop my class, as they felt they were at a disadvantage. Luckily, I was able to alleviate their fears, as I told them that they did not need technology at home to succeed in my class. In addition, I told them that their lack of experience with technology only makes it more necessary for them to be in a class with iPads. Other students did not understand why technology was a necessity in the classroom. Yes, students born in 1995 and 1996, students who have only known an Internet-connected culture, students who had their own iPhones in their pockets, asked why technology was necessary.

When students first reacted this way, I was dumbfounded; I did not expect the "Facebook generation" to question why we were using technology in the classroom. I always thought it would be *parents* who would reject the technology aspect of English class; I even anticipated this hesitation from parents and explained the technology and addressed it on my syllabus and website. As much as I thought parents would have questions, I never received phone calls about our yearlong adventure with technology. I did not expect such questions from my students.

As I am now able to reflect upon this experience with technology, I now know why some students were hesitant about the iPads. Some felt this way mainly because they did not know if they could succeed when they can't afford the technology and Internet at home. They were hiding their trepidation that their peers would become aware of their disadvantaged home life (which, of course, is all the more reason why they should be in a class that gives them experience with technology). As a result, they used whatever coping mechanisms they had to express their fear. In this case, it was questioning why it was needed.

There is a second reason why students held such caution about the technology. After 10 years of excellence in completing worksheets, writing essays, and using paper and pencil, I was now asking them to show their knowledge in new, creative ways. In retrospect, as much as I focused on how much the iPads would change the way I taught, I did not think about how startling it would be for students to be told that the way they have learned reading and writing for the past 10 years was about to completely change.

In truth, many students are comfortable with the way we have previously taught them, as testing has forced our students to simply regurgitate information or demonstrate basic reading comprehension. When presented with a device that forced them to create products and demonstrate comprehension beyond a true/false, multiple-choice question, students were surprisingly hesitant. They struggled with true creativity, and at times they failed miserably. Even to this day, when I assign activities, some students get extremely frustrated if an app is not easy to use. They react by begging for a worksheet or some alternative assignment to complete instead.

That is not to say that all students revolted against the iPads. In fact, only one or two students in each class questioned the technology while the majority impatiently asked when we would receive them. I just wish I would have known at the onset that not all students would be as enthusiastic about the technology as I was.

Designing Lessons to Teach Content and Meet the Four Cs

Whenever I hold PD or workshops for other educators, many ask how to design lessons to ensure that not only the four Cs are met, but class content is also taught and learned. To ensure that my students and I effectively use technology, every lesson follows the framework known as TPACK. Overall:

> Technological Pedagogical Content Knowledge (TPACK) attempts to identify the nature of knowledge required by teachers for technology integration in their teaching, while addressing the complex, multifaceted and situated nature of teacher knowledge. At the heart of the TPACK framework is the complex interplay of three primary forms of knowledge: Content (CK), Pedagogy (PK), and Technology (TK).
>
> (Koehler, 2012)

When educators teach their content using pedagogically sound practices that incorporate technology in a meaningful manner, they have reached the middle of the Venn diagram (Figure 1.2). To simplify, TPACK states that, to effectively integrate technology in the classroom, teachers must first possess expertise with their content. This is known as content knowledge. This is logical. After all, how can students learn class content if the teacher does not understand it? The next circle, pedagogical knowledge, states that teachers must have knowledge in how to teach that content, or sound pedagogical methods/strategies.

The overlapping of these two circles is known as pedagogical content knowledge. This is effective instruction with regard to 20th-century learning. We, as teachers, have been trained to understand and teach our content using effective methods in our classrooms in hopes that students will understand it.

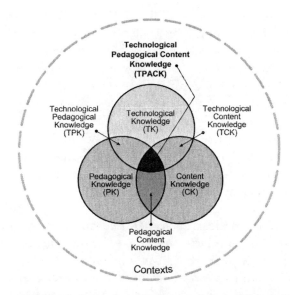

FIGURE 1.2 Technological Pedagogical Content Knowledge (TPACK)

However, we now live in the 21st century, and technology must now play a role in instruction on a regular basis. Thus, after a teacher possesses expertise in both content and knows effective methods of how to teach it, the third circle of the triple Venn diagram is introduced: technological knowledge. Teachers must find the appropriate tools that they and their students can use to enhance the instruction and learning of class content. When all three are combined, a teacher effectively uses technology in lessons to teach the content in meaningful and various ways.

This is a logical approach to technology, and it works for me. I keep this framework in mind when lesson-planning because it helps keep my focus on the delivery of content with technology, not just technology. If my lesson does not encompass all three parts of the Venn diagram or focuses too much on the technology aspect, I need to go back to the drawing board and redesign the lesson.

The way in which I lesson-plan using the TPACK framework, and technology, involves three parts. I plan with this process:

1. I figure out the content I need to teach. This is aligned to the Common Core Content Standards and pacing guides.

2a. I figure out exactly how I want to teach the content. I think of activities and tools that will introduce the content and specific standard(s) to my students.

2b. I think of apps and Web tools that both students and I can use to enhance the delivery of content. I incorporate this into the lesson.

3. I think of and implement apps and Web tools that students can use to show me that they understand the content and standard(s) just taught (usually some type of formative assessment). I incorporate it into the lesson.

In addition, my district uses learning targets to focus each individual lesson on a specific skill that students are to master. This is helpful, as these targets are student-friendly statements that show students what they need to know by the end of the class period. They also allow me to focus my lessons on one or two key standards and assess based on those concepts alone with apps and tools.

I find that if, after lesson-planning, I am using technology as an aid in the teaching, learning, and assessment of that learning target, then I am following the TPACK method. If my lesson focuses too much on technology, and I am not able to formatively assess whether or not students learned the lesson's target with regard to the Common Core, I need to adjust my lesson to do so.

At first, I struggled, especially in creating lessons with the devices. During my first year with the iPads, I can remember weeks at a time in which the iPads stayed in their carts as I focused on worksheets and other tried-and-true methods. When crafting lessons, I had to remain fully aware of the device. Otherwise, I would forget to incorporate it into my plans. As a result, I had to be more creative and open to apps that students could use. It was not until my second year with the technology that planning the iPad into each lesson became second nature.

When it comes to lesson-planning, the most important piece of advice I can give is to spend time researching, downloading, and exploring apps and Web tools that you potentially want to use in your classroom. Many of the websites that I use to find new apps are highlighted at the end of this book. Then, when you lesson-plan and have an app that you want to use, figure out how it works and utilize it only when it will complement the lesson/standard at hand.

Building an arsenal of apps to use for lessons takes time and change takes time. If you are lesson-planning and can't find a tool to use on the device, there is nothing wrong with not using the iPad that day. The iPad should be used to enrich the learning of your content. It is not appropriate for an activity if it does not support the learning of your content.

Conclusion

As teachers, we are educating in a time in which the outside world is progressing as our classrooms are quickly becoming stagnant. With technology in students' hands, we can help create experiences that will open our students' eyes to new tools, apps, and websites that can help foster the different parts of the Partnership for 21st Century Skills Framework and teach Common Core Standards. This will not only help students to learn the reading and writing skills they need when they leave high school, but it will better prepare students to become college- and career-ready, as technology is more abundant in college and in the workforce.

With critical thinking, communication, collaboration, and creativity in mind, it only makes sense that students are using technology in the classroom just as much as their teachers, if not more. However, as much as technology is stressed in schools today, it will never be truly valued until we have assessments that force students to become critical thinkers and to create innovative products.

These new ways of using technology open the door to teach the four Cs that students need to succeed outside of the classroom in a world riddled with technology. While I still have a lot of work to do before I completely meet all components of the Framework for 21st Century Learning, I have found that by crafting lesson that follow the TPACK model, along with activities utilizing the four Cs, I am not only teaching my content in an innovative manner, but I am also crossing over into other areas of P21's framework and giving students the skills they truly need.

But the underlying theme of technology and this new time in education is that it forces not only students, but teachers to learn and grow together in ways we could never have guessed 10 years ago. In such a short span of time, my students and the iPads have taught me more about innovative, effective, and engaging pedagogical methods than any professor or professional development opportunity ever has. Technology forces *everyone* to constantly learn, create, and ultimately grow in the classroom, not just students. When it comes to the future of education, the fact that *everyone* is constantly learning something new and growing each day might just be the most exciting idea of all.

2

Classroom Management and Essential Rules for Using iPads

10 Essential Rules for Management

From the time I learned my students and I would use iPads in the classroom, I had a vision of what the first day with them would be like. Students were so excited about their arrival that I knew instruction would be superfluous; I would delay my lesson and give them a full class period to be explorers. I envisioned first telling my students the rules for using the iPads. They would then anxiously grab their assigned iPad and follow all the rules I had just outlined. Some would surf the Web, some would browse through the apps, and others would experiment with the Camera Roll. They would be like Christopher Columbus, exploring this new, uncharted world and informing me of new tools they had just discovered. At the end of the day, they would put their iPad back in the assigned slot, smile at me, and wave goodbye. I was going to single-handedly change the face of education and engage students in ways they never knew existed.

And then reality hit. When the bell for each period rang, I outlined my rules for using the iPad for the first 10 minutes of class. I addressed expectations and potential issues such as theft, straying off task, and not following directions. During this time, I might as well have talked to a wall, as most of my students spent this time exchanging glances at me at the front of the room with the iPad cart at the back of the room. We have all experienced that time when we are talking to our students and feel as if no one is listening to us. I should have known this was just foreshadowing the behavior to come.

After explaining my rules, I assigned students numbers. There were 30 numbered iPads in one cart. I gave each student their number for the year, and sent them to the back of the room in groups of 10 to retrieve their number.

As they grabbed the device for the first time, I noticed that students had their individual reactions to the device. Some students gladly opened it up and sifted through the tools. Others carefully opened the cover and tellingly showed that they had never held a tablet before in their lives, as they had no idea how to flip through the screens. Some commented on how much money was now in our classroom, clearly uncomfortable with the value of the device they had in their hands. For the first few periods, everything went well, and students explored the device they would use for the whole year.

Then, problems started to arise. Around the middle of that first day, students found the Camera Roll and started to experiment with it. They took distorted images with the Photo Booth feature, and some students informed me of inappropriate photos in the Camera Roll from prior class periods. These photos broke about three of the rules I had set.

Reality had hit and I was utterly disappointed. I was disappointed in the guilty students, I was disappointed in myself, and I was disappointed that the first day was tarnished with such a lack of respect for the technology and how it should be used. It ruined my first day teaching with the iPads; I had hoped my students would appreciate the technology and follow the directions I specifically laid out for them. After all, I had just outlined exactly how to use the devices appropriately. I was crushed. At the end of the day, I wondered why some students did not listen to me.

While my students were enthralled with this technology in the classroom, up until now, they only knew how to use it for entertainment purposes. They did not know of the plethora of apps available to *learn*. They were only aware of what was available for leisure, as this was how they used their phones, iPods, and other devices. This was something I did not anticipate; therefore, I spent the next day discussing the photos that were taken and explaining that the iPads were to be used strictly for educational purposes. Additionally, it's important to discuss with students the importance of leaving a positive digital footprint; once something is published on the Web, it can be there forever. Luckily, in the case of these photos on the Camera Roll, the classroom environment made for a safe place for students to learn from their mistakes.

While the guilty students definitely have ownership in the issue, I also made mistakes that first day. In hindsight, I can honestly say my expectations were way too high. I thought that, along with changing my instruction, the iPads would turn my students into perfect little explorers. The truth is, teenagers are not perfect and make mistakes. Nothing will ever change this, not even offering an iPad in their hands. While technology offers a new facet to teaching and learning in my classroom, it will not keep students on task unless there is an efficient structure and management system in place for their use. Thus, giving them a full class period to explore without any educational activity was a giant mistake on my part.

I also made the mistake that teachers often make in their first year of teaching. I dwelled on the two students who broke the rules. I did not celebrate the fact that 128 other students followed my directions. Outside of these two students' mistakes, the first day was actually quite successful, and almost all students followed directions.

What I did not know at the time was what a blessing my students' and my own mistakes were and how it would impact the rest of the school year. After viewing the photos, I responded swiftly and wrote referrals to the office for the guilty students; they were sent to the office, given detentions, and banned from the devices for two weeks. This, as a result, set the tone and had an immediate effect on the rest of my classes. Students knew, right from the first day, if they were to disobey the rules, I would find out, discipline them, and ban them from the iPad for a lengthy period of time. The punished parties did not enjoy bringing their heavy textbooks to class. As their peers swiped through the pages of their online textbooks with glee, the guilty leafed through the mountain of pages in the book in front of them.

Disabling the Camera Roll after this incident also established a strict environment with the devices; it showed all students that anything can be disabled on their iPads if they demonstrate that they do not have the maturity to use it in an educational manner. This action, along with punishing the guilty parties, helped to create a climate of respect for the devices, and students knew I could and would take away any tool on the iPad. It set the tone in the classroom, and students knew that I would follow through with my word. All teachers know that follow-through is an important aspect of effective classroom management. It works when incorporating technology usage in the classroom as well.

The rules I laid out also contributed to the respect of the devices. Posted in the front of my classroom, these are 10 rules I use to ensure students use the devices the way they are supposed to be used. They have helped me to manage my classroom effectively. I added to this list of rules throughout the school year as different issues were brought to my attention. Posted in the front of my classroom and in my syllabus, these 10 rules encompass anything and everything to manage a 21st-century classroom effectively with any technological device (Figure 2.1).

FIGURE 2.1 iPad rules

Rule 1: Once You Grab Your Device out of the Cart, Inspect it and Inform Me of Any Abuse

My classroom routine is set up like this: each day, when students walk into my classroom, they are to go to the iPad cart, grab their device, and inspect it (Figure 2.2). If anything is wrong with the device, whether it fails to turn on, the screen is cracked, or they discover inappropriate photos, apps, or websites, they tell me right when they find it. If they do not tell me about anything inappropriate or missing and the person in the class after them finds it, the blame falls on the person who used it last. This ensures that I address any issue with the appropriate student.

At first, I did not think my students would inform me of any abuse; after all, nobody likes a tattletale. I was shocked when students informed me of everything, from the eventual wear and tear from being taken out of the cart to the supposed inappropriate Google searches of the Salem Witchcraft Trials. This was due to the fact that the consequences I set in place were pretty harsh and the fact that I would follow through with the consequences. If students were caught doing something inappropriate, they lost the privilege for at least a week. They also had to bring their textbook to class, and if you have seen the size of an English textbook, you'll know this alone is a punishment.

I also gave students time before the bell rang to use the iPad for entertainment purposes. A benefit to this change in routine was that students started to arrive to class early to play with the device. They would grab the device, inspect it, and then peruse through apps or websites. Once the bell rang, it was time to use the device to strengthen our reading and writing skills. I also noticed that students who normally used the restroom before class or strolled in late started to arrive to class early to use their iPad. Part of this was the fact that if a student came into class late with no pass, they could not use their iPad that day.

FIGURE 2.2 iPad cart

Rule 2: No Inappropriate Photos, Texts, Comments, etc.

One of the first features students found on the iPad was the Camera Roll. Students loved the Camera Roll and wanted to take pictures and videos of everything around them. In addition, they enjoyed using Photo Booth and created various distorted photos of themselves. They loved taking pictures of themselves and one another. As long as they are not inappropriate, I do not have a problem with it as long as it is during downtime such as before class.

Due to our school's policy and the fact that some students did not sign a permission slip to be photographed or videotaped, I created an addendum to this rule later on in the school year. Students were to first ask before taking a video or picture of another person. This not only teaches students to be courteous digital citizens, but in our school, students must sign a form to be filmed or to have their photo taken. Thus, a good rule of thumb is to ask an administrator for a list of students whose parents did not sign off on the photo/video agreement form.

Because these students could not use the Camera Roll or be photographed, for any assignment that required the tool, I typically gave the students a modified assignment. Or, I would give them the same assignment and grade them on a script of what they would have filmed had they been able to film it. This did not really create extra work on my end; out of 130 students spread across six classes, only one student did not turn in their photo release statement. At the beginning of the school year, after all paperwork has been turned into the office, I would ask an administrator for this list, as you must adhere to it. You do not want a student to be filmed against the parents' wishes.

For some students, the camera became so distracting that I restricted it from certain iPads. You can restrict it by click on the Settings feature on each iPad and turning the feature off. Once you do this, the only way in which the camera can appear on that iPad is to type in a four-number pass code that students can't access.

It is important to note that, for certain apps, such as iMovie, students will need to have the Camera Roll enabled or Location Services (also accessible in the Settings) turned on to import pictures and videos. This is a frequently asked question by students. Thus, it is important to be aware of how to enable this feature for certain apps.

In addition, in some chat rooms or discussion threads, such as Neat Chat, students have the ability to type in a name or nickname. Fellow teachers warned me about students using inappropriate nicknames whenever they used communication/collaboration tools. To keep this from happening, for any tool we used in which students could create a nickname, I asked them to type their first name and last initial.

Rule 3: Ask Three and Then Ask Me

There will be times, depending on the lesson or activity, when students will have a lot of questions about their device. One of the first things I showed my students was how to reconnect to the Internet once they have lost Internet access.

This is, without a doubt, the most common question that pops up. At first, I was pretty patient and helped students reconnect; however, as the year progressed, students became ruder about their lack of Internet access. Sometimes, I would lecture, all 30 iPads would lose connectivity to the internet at the same time, everybody would look up from their devices completely bewildered, and many would interrupt, "I have no Internet," unaware that five people had just said the same phrase right before them. It can make for a frustrating experience when you are trying to teach hyperbole and thousands of voices are complaining about their lack of connectivity to the Web.

After these outbursts became all too familiar, I knew I needed to change the routine, as scolding my students for these outbursts was not working. I not only wanted to eliminate these disruptions, but I also wanted my students to use problem-solving skills. In addition, I could not afford to take 10 minutes out of class each day to help students reconnect to the Internet. I decided to create a rule an elementary teacher told me about that he calls "ask three, then ask me." The way it works is simple; if a student experiences trouble with the device, he or she can quietly ask the person sitting next to him or her for help. If, after asking three people, the student is still having trouble, he or she can raise his or her hand and ask me for help. This created a calmer atmosphere, as students collaborated with one another for help. I noticed once I implemented this rule that I experienced fewer interruptions during my lessons.

It best serves anyone reading this book to be realistic; the technology is going to fail both you and your students during the course of the school year. I can't stress enough, though, to have a strategy and routine for students to follow when they are experiencing difficulties with the technology. This rule works for me because I do not mind students quietly helping one another with technology-related issues during my instruction, just as long as it does not take that long to fix. The "ask three" rule allows me to keep teaching without interruptions, and it helps me to keep my sanity.

Rule 4: Do Not Connect to Your iTunes Account

One question that students ask is if they can use their own personal Apple IDs to log in to their account and download apps. Early on in the process of using the iPads, I was unaware that students could access their own iTunes accounts from each iPad. Thus, I was surprised when apps that I had never even heard of showed up on the iPads. Once I found out about this, I then decided to ban any personal iTunes accounts from the class set of iPads. I strongly advise using this rule so that games and other apps do not end up on the iPad without your knowledge. This ensures that only approved, school-appropriate apps are bought and downloaded onto each iPad. I also check each iPad on a biweekly basis to make sure everything is school-appropriate.

Rule 5: Stay on Task at All Times

This rule is an obvious one, but at first it was difficult to manage. Students are pretty sneaky; they know how to break some rules in a stealthy fashion.

At the onset of this experience, as we read aloud as a class or completed other activities on the iPad, it was extremely easy for students to check entertainment websites instead of learn. This was especially true when I was in the front of the classroom controlling the interactive whiteboard and all the iPad screens faced away from me.

This is where rule 1 comes in handy; students will tattletale on one another in fear of losing their privileges. At the beginning of the year, many students informed me of other students who were checking personal Twitter accounts instead of completing an assigned task. As students understood that I would give consequences for being off task, I found that fewer students used these types of sites in class. Therefore, rule 1 helps enforce this rule.

When I told a particular student that he or she was banned, I first showed them a screenshot of the abuse, as I took a picture of it, and I then told them to start bringing their textbook. When the week was over (depending on the severity, sometimes it was more than a week), I would tell them they could start using their iPad again.

As the year progressed, I found a way to teach throughout the classroom and not just at the front. This way, I could monitor the iPad screens as I taught. The app is called Splashtop. It is well worth the money. With Splashtop, I am able to control my desktop using the iPad. I simply type in a username and password I create on Splashtop's website into the iPad, and my desktop computer appears (Figure 2.3). As a result, I rarely use my MimioBoard; I can walk around the classroom, control my desktop, and monitor students' screens. I am no longer confined to the front of the room. This makes classroom management much easier, as I can view what is on each screen as I walk around the room. I would not hesitate to purchase the app. Just keep in mind that you will need to create a Google e-mail account to set it up.

FIGURE 2.3 Splashtop

There are other apps similar to Splashtop available in the App Store. I have found similar ones such as RemoteMouse and Doceri Desktop. However, my school's filter blocks many of these apps from connecting to my desktop. I bought Splashtop because my school has permitted its access through our filter. Test out the free apps or check with your school's media specialist or technology coordinator before you spend any money on this type of app. If the free apps work in your district, I would not spend any money on Splashtop.

Eventually, I switched from Splashtop to Apple TV. Apple TV, when used with a projector with HDMI capabilities, allows users to project their iPad screen. I have found this to be even better than Splashtop, as I can show students how to use a certain app before they begin an activity. It also makes uploading documents and videos much easier, as students can complete steps with me as I do it by looking at my projected iPad screen. In addition, I have more mobility around the classroom and can teach from anywhere. For certain lessons in which I need my Windows desktop, though, I will revert back to Splashtop.

Rule 6: Stick with Your School E-mail Account, Not Personal Accounts

Many students have their own personal e-mail accounts, and the iPad presents a life skill we can teach our students. Many students want to use their personal e-mails when creating accounts, as many accounts ask for an e-mail address. I discourage students from doing this, as it is generally beneficial to use personal e-mails for home use and professional e-mail addresses for school use. Students need to learn this skill as well, as many of them are unaware of it. They need to leave home at home and use school e-mail on a school device.

Thus, I have my students use the e-mail address that our school provides. It ensures that they are able to verify accounts, use the same e-mail and password in the creation of all accounts, and easily remember these e-mails and passwords. I do not have any issues with students forgetting their usernames or passwords; usernames are typically their e-mail addresses and passwords are their lunch codes they use to buy lunch each day in the cafeteria.

Rule 7: When I say iPads Closed, Close its Cover

"iPads closed" is one of the new catchphrases our great team picked up since using them in the classroom. I learned early on in the process that students want to look at their iPads when I am giving directions or during live discussions, unaware of how rude it is. While it is not exactly shocking, it became a nuisance.

Therefore, when I am talking and want undivided attention, I will simply say, "iPads closed," or "eyes and ears." This lets them know that if I do not have their undivided attention, they will risk being banned from the iPad. It is a simple signal that lets them know I want their undivided attention, and it works well.

Rule 8: Log Out When You are Finished with a Site

Throughout the course of a week, I will hear about three or four times that someone did not log out of an app or website. I imagine that for every student that speaks up about someone not logging off, there are quite a few others who say nothing about it.

Obviously, this rule is meant to protect students. Bullying is an issue today; the last thing I want to occur in my classroom is for a student's account to be left open and false information to spread about that student throughout the school. Fortunately, I have not encountered a situation that has resulted in bullying.

Even though this is a rule, many students have a difficult time remembering to follow it. There are times, at the end of class, when students are so caught up in completing an assignment that they forget to log out of the app or website. I can't really blame them; they are accustomed to using their own phones and other personal devices in which they do not need to log out.

I found that posting the words "log off" on worksheets and on the board helps. Other than that, this is a rule that many students struggle to follow, especially when the bell rings, and they are under pressure to finish an assignment and get to their next class.

As my school prepares to go 1:1 and students have their own devices, this will not be an issue. However, I always tell my students to politely log the last person off if they forgot to do so. I remind them that, if they were in the same situation, they would want the next user to do so for them. Overall, this logic tends to work with students, and I have not had an issue with students abusing others' accounts.

Rule 9: Bring Your Own Device in at Your Own Risk

This is more of a school rule, but it is still one that I use in my class as well. Our school district, upon preparation for mobile devices, changed its policy and allowed all students to bring in and use their own mobile devices in the school.

About three to four students in each of the six classes I teach bring in their iPads on a daily basis. In my syllabus, I inform parents that students who bring in their own devices do so at their own risk; they should not feel compelled to bring in their own devices, as I can provide them with one.

I establish this rule for two reasons. For one, I want to inform parents how I intend to utilize the technology and that it will be used to enhance the learning process. Second, I want to protect myself. None of my students has lost his or her device or been victims of theft, but if that day ever occurs, I like to have documentation that states it was never necessary for students to bring in their own devices.

Rule 10: Respect the Opportunity to Use the Technology

My last rule for students is one that sums up all of the other nine rules; I simply want them to look at this as an opportunity. As I travel and speak to other educators about technology, I realize what a gift and rare opportunity these mobile devices afford my students. I want my students to realize this as well.

Thus, the day before we begin using the iPads, I discuss this opportunity with my students. I ask students what it means to respect the opportunity. At first, students have a difficult time answering this question. By the end of the discussion, however, they understand what I want them to learn: respecting the technology means using it the way it is meant to be used in the classroom. While they can be used to entertain, iPads should be used in class to learn.

In addition, this rule also helps if a student does something inappropriate with the iPad that the other rules do not address. I will not pretend to know everything that the iPad can do; thus, I do not pretend to know everything a student can do on the iPad. Thus, if some new problem appears or if a student does something inappropriate that rules 1–9 do not address, I can always use rule 10 as a backup.

Consequences

As with any breaking of the rules, I discipline my students depending on the behavior. When I catch a student abusing the iPad, I take it away from him or her immediately and tell the culprit to use a pen and paper and to begin bringing his or her textbook. If the offense is completely inappropriate, I send the student to the office and ban that student for a length of time ranging from a week to a month. For most minor infractions, such as not paying attention or surfing the Web at an inappropriate time, I typically scold the student, give a detention, and ban him or her for a week. If I have to scold the student a second time, I will ban him or her for two weeks and call home. All in all, I use my own discretion; each consequence depends on each individual offense.

Other Tips for Day-to-Day Success

Based on experiences with the iPads, there are some strategies that have contributed to day-to-day success. These include:

- Teach students how to connect and reconnect to the Internet on day one; have them actually do it themselves.
- Have a backup plan in your head in case an app is unreliable or the Internet is unavailable.
- Know how to use a tool before you use it in a lesson; do not assume all students know how to use it.
- Assign an individual background for each iPad and tell students not to change the background; this way, students will know it's their iPad once they open it. If they have a different background, they will know it's not their iPad they grabbed from the cart.
- Make sure an e-mail account is attached to each iPad (some assignments will need to be e-mailed to you).

- If students are creating a product, make sure they have a way to share it with you to view and assess (two great options are e-mail and uploading it to a Schoology course).

- If an app is not working correctly, resetting the iPad generally works (select a reset option in which media and content will *not* be deleted).

Conclusion

All in all, posting and following rules has created a classroom environment in which students respect the technology, lessons run more smoothly, and everyone is accountable for their actions. I cannot stress enough that these rules work because of the consequences I have set in place when they are broken. Teenagers mess up; they are not perfect. The technology does not magically turn them into perfect angels who will listen to me every minute of every lesson. Along with these rules, my students know my expectations and that I will follow through with consequences if these expectations are not met. In this one way, my classroom management routine has stayed true to the way it was before the iPads arrived. The biggest difference is that I have more to manage.

3

Redefining the Teacher Website

When I first prepared to use iPads, I wanted to create an all-new teacher website that students would actually visit on a regular basis. If your students are like mine, they rarely go to a class website unless absolutely necessary. I initially thought the iPads would make my teacher website more interactive than ever before. I found an easy-to-use website maker, Weebly. It's an easy tool to use; users can simply drag and drop different elements onto a page to create a website. There is no need for HTML lingo to create a website.

Thus, I created a teacher website that had a lot of features. I was able to upload special features such as videos and audio files for students to view. I even told my students at the beginning of the year that they would be uploading assignments via this website that would directly forward to my e-mail account.

The Pitfalls of a Teacher Website

But by the time we reached the middle of the school year, I had completely abandoned this website. In theory, it was a great idea. I had each class set up as a tab. I uploaded student examples. I had MLA resources and instructional videos. However, this website failed to work for a few reasons. First, it was not entirely compatible with the iPad. This is a problem with many online website creators. I wanted my students to upload their own videos and other files via the iPad. They could not do so with Weebly, as many of Weebly's features are not compatible with the iPad. The only way in which the website could be updated was through a desktop or laptop. Thus, my website, like other websites I have tried to create in the past, went on the back burner.

There is another reason many of us are not using teacher websites to the fullest potential. Due to the fact that they are a supplemental element to the classroom, they are often forgotten by both teachers and students. The problem is that they are not used with day-to-day instruction. For me, each school year begins the same way. I create a website. But then, by the time October hits, I am spending so much time trying to create meaningful lessons and keep up with grading that I simply have little to no time to update a website. As a result, I abandon the website. At the risk of sounding like a lazy teacher, I simply do not have time to update a website on a regular basis throughout a school year. While it was quite interactive and informative, it was not a tool both my students and I could easily use *inside* the classroom on a daily basis with the iPads.

Schoology and Social Networking for the Classroom

Then, a colleague introduced Schoology to me. Schoology is a learning management system that allows for true collaboration within the classroom. Think of it as Facebook for the classroom. It has quite a few features that make it great for both teachers and students to use.

Schoology is very similar to Facebook, only it is geared toward educational use. Most of my students have a Facebook page, and introducing a similar website in the classroom is fairly easy. Students understand the basics of the site. They create an account using their school e-mail (every student in our district has a school-issued e-mail address) and they create their own password. I suggest that they keep all of their usernames and passwords the same; they use their school e-mail addresses for usernames and their passwords are their numeric lunch codes. This makes it easier for students to keep track of their username and password for every account they create in class, as they are all the same.

Once they log in, Schoology takes them to a home page. Just like Facebook, the home page provides students with a newsfeed. It lets them know recent posts by people in any of their groups or by the instructor in any of their courses. This is an excellent way for students to stay up-to-date with assignments. I can remind students of an essay or other homework that is due, and once they log in to Schoology, the message is right there waiting for them right in their newsfeed.

Creating Courses

Schoology allows teachers to create courses for all of the classes they teach. Creating a course is extremely easy. All I do is click on the "Course" tab, click "Create Course," and then type in the period information for that class. From there, I can upload assignments, create online tests/quizzes, upload files/links, and create discussion boards, albums, and other different pages (Figures 3.1 and 3.2). It is truly a one-stop shop for teachers to post all their work online. It can also help create a paperless classroom, as students can send messages, download worksheets with apps, and submit papers onto the website from the iPad.

It is also easy for students to join your course, and they do so on the first day of class. All they need to do is click on the "Courses" tab and click "Join." From there, they type in an access code that I provide. The access code, only issued to the instructor of a course, is highlighted on the course home page (Figure 3.3). This access code will then take students to the home page where they can view assignments, links, and discussions.

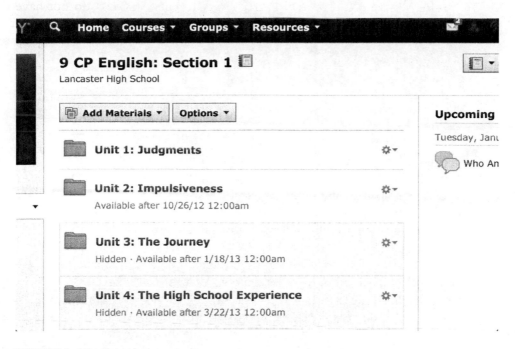

FIGURE 3.1 Schoology course page

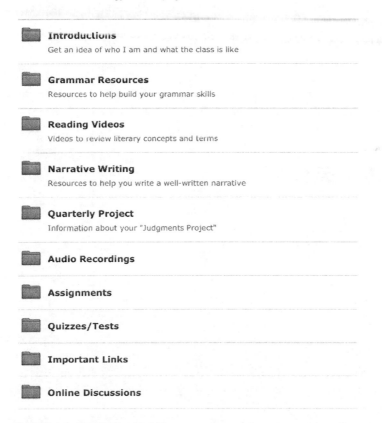

FIGURE 3.2 Schoology unit folder

FIGURE 3.3 Schoology course access code

I have set up courses for each of the six class periods I teach. Unlike past websites, I have been successful in updating these course pages because, first, it is easy to upload assignments, and second, it is integrated into my lessons each day. Each student can log into Schoology, go to my course under the "Courses" tab, and then open up whatever attachments go along with that day's assignment or lesson.

An easy way to start creating assignments is to have students open up PDF attachments from Schoology with the app Type on PDF. To do so, I convert particular worksheets to a PDF. The process to do so is fairly simple. When saving a file in Microsoft Word, I save it as a PDF in the "Save as Type" feature. This is located under the space where you type the name of the file. From there, I upload the file into Schoology as an assignment. From there, students click and hold the attachment link, and then they select "Open with Type on PDF." Afterwards, students write on the document and send it to me via e-mail or upload it to Schoology for me to grade (Figure 3.4). It's an easy way to update the old-fashioned worksheet.

I like the Type on PDF app, and to be honest, there are many other PDF file annotation apps available in Apple's app store. Type on PDF does come in both free and paid versions. I use the paid version to view and grade my students'

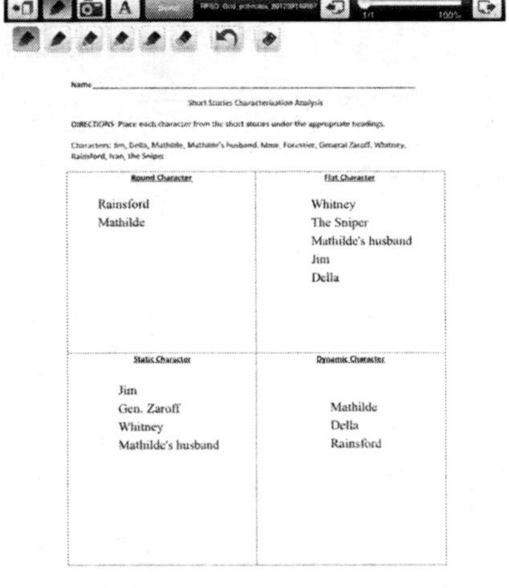

FIGURE 3.4 Worksheet completed using Type on PDF

files while my students use the free version to annotate worksheets and send them to me via e-mail.

Schoology courses are also great for absent students. I have eliminated the "Absence Folder" and simply tell students to check Schoology if they are absent. I am able to post each day's assignments and upload notes, links, files, movies, audio, and anything else pertaining to my lessons. Students no longer need to ask for absence work; it is waiting for them on Schoology. This is because I post the assignments (I can even post videos of assignments, telling students in a video what their task is for the day) for each day on Schoology, and students open them up in class to watch them. All in all, because I have made the website a part of my instructional practices, it has made me more diligent in keeping our Schoology course updated, as it is an essential part of my lesson-planning.

When it comes to setting up a course, I like to organize it using my own folders and tabs. Schoology comes with default tabs for assignments, quizzes, albums, files, discussions, and pages, but I hide these default folders and then create my own. Due to the fact that I teach primarily thematically, I organize my course into the four main folders pertaining to each quarter and its theme. From there, I have folders inside those units with different resources, assignments, discussion threads, and much more.

There are many other ways to organize courses. You can create courses for each particular unit, theme, grading period, genre, literary period, or even for each week of the school year. All in all, I find it best to create folders that relate to the way I teach the class.

Inside each unit's folder, I have numerous folders that relate to different activities. I have folders set up for assignments, online discussions, informational text discussions, tests, writing resources, reading resources, and instructional review videos (Table 3.1). From there, I upload attachments into those folders based around the Common Core Standards I teach that quarter. This is indicated in my school's pacing guide for that particular grade. There are many ways to organize each course. Experiment and find the way that works best for you.

Without a doubt, the greatest perk of Schoology is the ability to copy anything and everything to multiple courses. Thus, when I create a course for

TABLE 3.1 Schoology course folder ideas

Assignments
Discussions
Projects
Quizzes/Tests
Writing Resources
Grammar Resources
Reading Resources
Links to Audio Books/Videos on YouTube
Articles of the Week
Unit/Course Introduction
Lessons/Absent Work

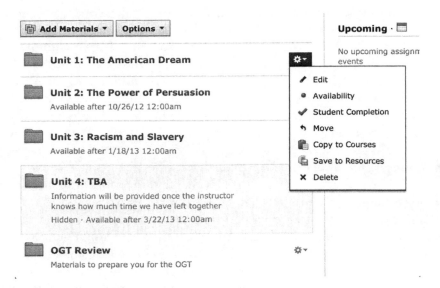

FIGURE 3.5 Copying course materials

a particular class, I create all the course content and folders for one particular section of a course. From there, I copy the course so that other sections of the same prep have the same material (Figure 3.5). For example, I teach three sections of English 10 CP. I only had to spend time creating one course for all three classes. This is due to the fact that I was able to copy the course twice and rename them to correspond to the period.

As a result of the "copy" function, I only had to create the course once to have it ready for three class periods or sections of that same prep. I can do the same thing for assignments, discussions, quizzes, tests, and everything else. Thus, instead of having to go to visit each individual section of a course to upload the same attachment or activity, I simply have to click "copy to course," select the appropriate folder, and it will be waiting for my students in other course sections. This saves so much time.

Even more, once a Schoology course has ended, the course then goes into an archive of past courses. I can visit these past courses at any time. I look at this as an updated way of keeping track of lesson plans; it is almost as if it has replaced my lesson-planning book, as each year I can look back at each course and see exactly how I taught different concepts, attachments, quizzes, discussions, and assignments. I can even take effective products students have created and use them as exemplars for future classes.

Creating Groups

Schoology also has a feature for teachers to create group pages for students. It is similar to the course page, but it is more geared toward group work. Creating a group is similar to creating a course. After creating a group, I can give my students in that group the access code to it. From there, members in the group can hold discussions, share information, and upload files (Figure 3.6). Due to the fact that I create the groups, I am the administrator (as highlighted by the crown next to my name in the group). I am able to monitor these groups and ban anyone who is abusing the privilege.

These groups allow for students to communicate and collaborate (two of the 21st Century skills) outside of the classroom in a monitored online environment. They can organize their group, delegate tasks, and have meaningful conversations about their projects. Students are highly engaged by this new way of contributing to group work; based on the fact that they are "schoologizing" (it'll become a catchphrase one day) well beyond the school day illustrates their interest in the website.

I have used Schoology groups primarily for large group projects, primarily those grounded in project-based learning. If I know that students will be in these groups for at least an extended period of time, I will create Schoology groups and give students the access code. If students are working in a group for a day or two and the project will be completed primarily in class, Schoology groups are not necessary.

FIGURE 3.6 Schoology group discussion

Even more, Schoology groups also offer an innovative way for *teachers* around the nation to collaborate with one another. Teachers can create groups to discuss different aspects of education with other teachers. In the past year, I have joined groups such as Flipped Classrooms, Schoology Educators, Language Arts, and 1 to 1 Computing. These groups have allowed me to find new ways to use Schoology, find new apps to use, find professional development opportunities relating to technology, and explore different lessons/resources of different Schoology educators around the country. Many teachers will share their resources for their classes with teachers in different groups. It has truly changed the way I collaborate; I now have access to how teachers across the United States are using technology in their respective classrooms. Many are willing to collaborate with one another. If you have any questions about how to use Schoology or if you have a problem, members in these groups are quick to help.

Discussions, Blogs, and Private Messaging

With Schoology, I have also changed the way I hold discussions in my classroom.

With threaded discussions, I can post a question about last night's reading, and from there, they can respond to that question (Figure 3.7). This allows me to assess whether or not students read and if they understood what they read. Students are pretty honest in these discussions; they do not hold back. They can also respond to one another; I usually invite them to respond to one another's thoughts, as long as they are doing so in a respectful and appropriate manner.

Schoology also allows students to private message me, but I typically do not use this function in my classroom. Quite frankly, I am just not comfortable with

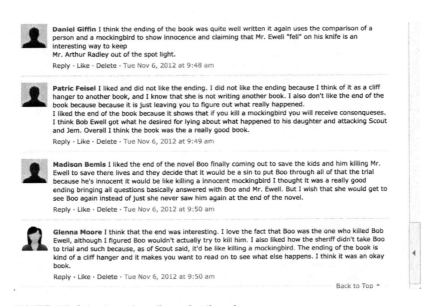

Daniel Giffin I think the ending of the book was quite well written it again uses the comparison of a person and a mockingbird to show innocence and claiming that Mr. Ewell "fell" on his knife is an interesting way to keep
Mr. Arthur Radley out of the spot light.
Reply · Like · Delete · Tue Nov 6, 2012 at 9:48 am

Patric Feisel I liked and did not like the ending. I did not like the ending because I think of it as a cliff hanger to another book, and I know that she is not writing another book. I also don't like the end of the book because because it is just leaving you to figure out what really happened.
I liked the end of the book because it shows that if you kill a mockingbird you will receive consonqueses. I think Bob Ewell got what he desired for lying about what happened to his daughter and attacking Scout and Jem. Overall I think the book was the a really good book.
Reply · Like · Delete · Tue Nov 6, 2012 at 9:49 am

Madison Bemis I liked the end of the novel Boo finally coming out to save the kids and him killing Mr. Ewell to save there lives and they decide that it would be a sin to put Boo through all of that the trial because he's innocent it would be like killing a innocent mockingbird I thought it was a really good ending bringing all questions basically answered with Boo and Mr. Ewell. But I wish that she would get to see Boo again instead of just she never saw him again at the end of the novel.
Reply · Like · Delete · Tue Nov 6, 2012 at 9:50 am

Glenna Moore I think that the end was interesting. I love the fact that Boo was the one who killed Bob Ewell, although I figured Boo wouldn't actually try to kill him. I also liked how the sheriff didn't take Boo to trial and such because, as of Scout said, it'd be like killing a mockingbird. The ending of the book is kind of a cliff hanger and it makes you want to read on to see what else happens. I think it was an okay book.
Reply · Like · Delete · Tue Nov 6, 2012 at 9:50 am

Back to Top ^

FIGURE 3.7 Schoology class discussion thread

this private form of communication. I like all forms of social networking to be out in the open for everyone to see; I figure if students need to private message me, they can do so via e-mail, which is monitored by my district's technology department. I know of other teachers who use the private message tool and have had no issues with it, but it is simply a tool that I am not comfortable using in my classroom. If you are comfortable using it in your classroom, it's a great tool to use for exit tickets or quick formatives at the end of lessons.

Uploading Document, Video, and Audio Files

Schoology's app also allows students to upload documents for teachers to comment on and grade. If you want to have students upload documents for the teacher to view and grade, create an assignment in Schoology. From there, students can share their PDF, Word, Excel, and PowerPoint files from apps that allow sharing into the assignment's Dropbox. From the app that they are using, they simply need click the "Share" feature (the icon usually is an arrow pointing to the right) and then select the Schoology app. From there, they select the assignment to upload the file into, and submit it for me to view and grade.

This is a great feature, as students can submit their essays and papers to our Schoology course right from the iPad. I have used this for worksheets and short paragraph responses to reading selections. I have to admit, however, that I rarely use this function for submitting essays or full-length papers, as I find that I give the most effective feedback when I have an actual paper to write on in front of me. To be honest, I find grading on the iPad extremely awkward. Thus, for many essays, I will have students print them and hand them in. In addition, for any worksheet, I have asked students to complete them with the Type on PDF app; they can then e-mail them to me. Thus, this is a function that I do not use that often.

In addition to uploading documents, Schoology also allows students and teachers to upload video and audio files. As I became more experienced with the iPad and Schoology, I also uploaded videos I had made. Using Apple's iMovie, I created instructional videos for flipped and blended learning. I spent one summer creating two- to three-minute videos covering each standard. Some videos were tutorials on how to format papers in MLA format, others were a basic review of characterization, summarizing, foreshadowing, conflicts, and much more. I was able to create, upload, and place these files in Schoology under the files/links tab in the course. This allows students to review important concepts for their midterm/final exams and any other test they may have. I have also uploaded review videos for standardized tests for students to watch at any time. This ensures that students are reviewing important course content in a variety of manners.

One of my favorite ways to use Schoology is to have students upload their own videos and pictures using the Schoology app. They can upload from the iPad with the Schoology app, but students can't upload videos from the iPad via the website, www.schoology.com. Thus, whenever we upload videos to our course, I always tell students to use the app. Over the course of the school year, students have uploaded music videos, collages, movies, and more to our Schoology course pages.

As I allowed students to upload videos and photos, I initially feared that inappropriate files would find their way onto our Schoology pages. However, due to the fact that every single file students post has their names attached, this has not been an issue at all. If anything inappropriate is posted, I can easily delete it and reprimand whoever posted the content.

Tests and Quizzes

Even more, Schoology offers teachers the ability to create online tests and quizzes that students can then take online. Chapter 6 reviews how to create tests and quizzes, as well as some of the trouble that my students and I have encountered with it. All in all, Schoology allows students to take tests on the iPad that can then be submitted to the teacher and automatically graded, depending on the types of questions.

Grade Book and Attendance

Schoology does have the option for teachers to create a grade book and take attendance. It comes with standard features such as weighting grades, creating a +/− system, rounding, grading categories, and more. I do not use this primarily due to the fact that my school uses a different online grade book.

Schoology's grade book has the potential to save teachers hours of time, as once a quiz/test is set up, the results sync to the grade book after a student has completed it. In addition, teachers can also enable grading and comments for course assignments. Once a teacher has graded a course assignment in Schoology, those grades will then immediately go to the Schoology grade book once a point value has been assigned. You do not even have to add students to the grade book; once they join the course, they are automatically inserted into it.

The grade book features eliminate the statistical work of importing grades into a grade book; once a grade is given for an assignment, that point value goes right to the Schoology grade book, as long as the grade book has been set up. Instead of grading the assignment and then typing it into the grade book, Schoology eliminates the second step and will do it for you. This is, without a doubt, a fantastic feature of Schoology that can save many teachers precious time to complete other tasks.

Troubleshooting

Throughout the course of a school year, my students have encountered a couple of issues with Schoology. For one, the app can be temperamental at times; some students have had trouble logging into the app. The app will state that it is having trouble verifying the user's credentials. When this happens, first check to see if the username and password are correctly typed in.

If that does not work, I will typically delete the Schoology app from the iPad, access the iPad's App Store and reinstall the app. If they still cannot log into the app, I will then perform a general reset in the Settings of the iPad. With any of these methods, students have been able to log back into the app to use its features.

More importantly, Schoology has a help center website that can answer virtually any question a user might have. It gives guides for instructors, students, administrators, and parents. I can also pose a question to one of the educator groups. Schoology Educators is a great group to join as you navigate the world of Schoology. Between both resources, I can usually obtain an answer to any question.

Conclusion

One of the neatest aspects of Schoology is that, if used for an entire school year, students will have an archive of our school year; each discussion, posting, blog, update, video, picture, and project that we could possibly upload ended up on our Schoology page. This is quite beneficial to students. They can, over the course of the school year, review past assignments, other students' videos, and discussions, and review important class concepts. Parents can also see what we are doing in class as well. Furthermore, at the end of the year, students perused our course page and reminisced on past lessons and experiences that they otherwise may have forgotten.

Schoology truly creates an environment in which students can learn from one another and review concepts without having to stare at notes in a spiral notebook. It has helped tremendously in my quest for an innovative classroom; this is due to the fact that, unlike other teacher websites I have created for my classroom, Schoology has become a resource both my students and I use daily. It has become crucial for students to share products and upload them in an area for me to grade. It has allotted time for online discussions. Students take tests in my Schoology courses and can share files with one another. The website has definitely created a collaborative atmosphere and one in which students can truly learn together. There are so many other features to Schoology; what I have outlined is simply the basics. There is a calendar, polls, rubric creation, and so much more! It constantly updates with new features. The upgraded version also allows for more features and controls.

While this clearly seems like an advertisement for Schoology, there are other social networking websites and apps available to try. One of the first I found upon receiving the iPads was Edmodo. It is similar to Facebook, especially in design. In the end, I chose Schoology over Edmodo because it is simply what I prefer, and I find it easier to navigate. I especially enjoy that its staff constantly updates both its website and app versions with new features. The Schoology staff even surfs different teacher group pages to see what teachers are saying about the Schoology experience. They take that feedback to create updates that enhance its website and app. Regardless of what you select, if you select social networking as a companion to your instruction, select the website that works best for you and your students' needs.

4

Transforming Writing with iPads

The Common Core Standards dictate that we teach different forms of writing throughout the course of a school year. Thus, I try to have my students write at least one major essay each quarter. Within one year, students write a narrative, a persuasive essay, an analytical essay, and a research paper. By having students write in each of these genres at least once, I am able to address most, if not all, of the Common Core Standards in my instruction.

With the iPad, there are numerous apps students can use to write essays and demonstrate knowledge of the Common Core Writing Standards. However, I have found that while using these apps with my students, each individual app or tool has its unique features that users need to be aware of to successfully implement them in the classroom.

Digital Storytelling with Storybird and Toontastic

Standard: 10.W.3

Write narratives to develop real or imagined experiences or events using effective technique, well-chosen details, and well-structured event sequences.

Task: Writing a narrative

Tool: storybird.com

Before the iPads, my students and I would study short stories, discuss the plot curve, understand how to write dialogue, and review figurative language in preparation for writing a personal narrative that would demonstrate proficiency in all of these skills. Students would type out their narratives with a correct MLA format heading, as this is integral to teaching college-bound students.

But then, I discovered digital storytelling. Digital storytelling is the use of technological tools to tell a story. These stories can be told in numerous ways: comics, movies, picture books, music videos, and much more.

Our grant team was able to switch from traditional narrative to digital storytelling without even using the iPad, and you can as well if you have a computer lab at your school. At a workshop, my fellow grant recipients and I found a website called Storybird. It is a fantastic website that any K-12 ELA teacher can use.

Users can type up a narrative and use preloaded collections of artwork to accompany their pages. The artwork is quite sophisticated, and the end result is a professional-looking picture book that students can buy in as a PDF, a paperback book, and a hardcover book.

The final product looks professional (Figures 4.1–4.4). I will never revert back to a traditional pen-and-paper narrative, as digital storytelling creates a more personal and meaningful experience for students. While there are other tools available to use to create digital narratives, Storybird will always be my first choice because the end result is a narrative that some students have actually purchased (Table 4.1).

The Storybird narrative also highlights an important theme running throughout the course of our year with the iPads: the ability to publish writing for an online audience. Students, upon completion of their Storybird narrative, published their narrative onto the Storybird website. From there, students and other Storybird users could read their narratives on the Web and comment on them (Figure 4.5). We even spent an entire period of class having a gallery walk; students copied and pasted links to their Storybirds on our Schoology page. From there, we were able to click on them, read them, and comment on one another's published work.

FIGURE 4.1 Student Storybird

As the door opened with a ding of the bell, I could practically hear my stomach plummet through the floor boards, heavy with the weight of millions of butterflies. They walked in hand-in-hand and sat down at their usual table in the far corner of the restaurant beneath a dim hanging light with a strange picture on a stained glass shade. It reflected red and blue light onto their faces in a beautiful, but eerie way.

FIGURE 4.2 Student Storybird

They weren't your usual couple that would sit across from each other on dates. Instead they liked to sit right next to each other. All of this just made me want to throw my silverware at them and that just upset me more. These people have ruined my family's tradition for me forever.

FIGURE 4.3 Student Storybird

Sitting in this old restaurant, my family has come to Pizza Hut every Friday night for as long as I can remember. It's no surprise that every employee there knows all of us by name. When I was younger, my brother and I used to race each other to the juke box. I usually won, although it didn't matter much because we both always chose the same song. The Great Juke Box Race added to the fact that, at the tender age of about five, pizza was my favorite food, made Fridays the best day of the week for me. However, the trips became less and less enjoyable and more and more of an annoyance as I got older and my siblings and I started to argue more (also, the pizza wasn't all that good). Over the past two months, though, my Friday nights have gotten unbelievably worse. They've actually become down right torturous.

FIGURE 4.4 Student Storybird

TABLE 4.1 Digital storytelling tools

Sock Puppets (app)
Story Wheel (app)
iTellaStory (app)
Bookabi (app)
PictureBook (app)
Book Creator (app)

If you want students to share their Storybirds, it is important that, when they publish their narratives, they make their narratives public, not private. If not, when you try to open it up to grade, you will receive a message stating that the story is private and not available to read.

More importantly, Storybird is a safe place to publish writing. The Storybird staff constantly monitors comments by users. Negative comments can't be published; in fact, users can't even publish books with words such as "shut up." This G-rated censorship ensures that students will not read or publish inappropriate content.

Table 4.2 also highlights a rubric that can be used to assess my students' Storybird narratives. Overall, my method of grading primarily focused on whether or not students demonstrated proficiency of Common Core Writing Standards with regard to narrative writing. I made one subtle change to the rubric;

FIGURE 4.5 Storybird users' comments

I added an area to incorporate the illustrations and whether or not they contributed to the story.

As I was grading, I noticed students wrote with the same grammatical errors I would have otherwise received with paper and pencil or Microsoft Word. However, I did see student writing improve in a few areas. First, students wrote more than the typical five paragraphs I usually ask them to write. I asked students to write at least five paragraphs, and they should have at least one paragraph per page of their Storybird. Many students typed 10 Storybird pages or more; some even wrote more than 20 pages. In addition, during the process, students were often frustrated that many of the pieces of artwork in a collection did not match their collection. While they were initially frustrated, this ultimately became a teachable moment; students added more details to their narratives to make the available artwork match it. I received detailed narratives that were more fully developed than I had received in past years.

While not exactly the most conventional app, Toontastic is an alternative to Storybird and also offers a sophisticated product. Toontastic is an app in which students can select characters, a background, and move them to create a movie that tells a story (Figures 4.6 and 4.7). They can use music cues and speak into the iPad to create a movie of their narrative. It even provides students with a simplified version of the plot curve that they can use as a method of pre-writing as it has students follow the order of the plot curve to structure their narrative (Figure 4.8). The end result is a spectacular video.

TABLE 4.2 Narrative rubric

Narrative Standard	4 (Exemplary)	3 (Proficient)	2 (Below Standard)	1 (Marginal)	0 (No Attempt)
The narrative is fully developed and the writer takes time to develop the story (at least one paragraph per part of the plot curve).					
Narrative has sophisticated figurative language and sensory language.					
The narrative's artwork relates to the words written on each page and contributes to the story.					
The narrative's dialogue is meaningful and essential when used.					
The narrative has effective transitions and is appropriately paced.					
The narrative is written in first person and has a distinct voice.					
The writer's conclusion has a reflection of the events in the narrative.					
The narrative has correct grammar/spelling.					

FIGURE 4.6
Toontastic

FIGURE 4.7
Toontastic

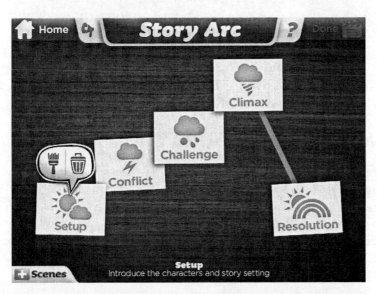

FIGURE 4.8
Toontastic plot diagram

CloudOn and Pages

Standard: 10.W.9

Draw evidence from literary or informational text to support analysis, reflection, and research.

Task: Writing an analytical essay

Tools: CloudOn, Pages

When I first received my iPads, one of most important apps I tried to find was a reliable word-processing app for the iPad. There are some, but they can be quite expensive; some cost up to $10–15. Quite frankly, these are too expensive to put on each iPad and are not completely reliable. Besides, apps are more fun when they are free.

By sticking to the free apps, I was able, either through my own research or colleagues sharing with one another, to find and use an app that allows students to use Microsoft Word on the iPad. The first app I heard about was CloudOn. While not a perfect app, CloudOn is quite reliable for word processing. It is easy to use. Once you open the app, you create an account and then it allows you to open up Microsoft Word, Excel, or PowerPoint (Figure 4.9). It saves your work automatically; there is no need to save at all. The reason why it does this is because your work saves to a cloud-based account. I usually ask students to use Dropbox, as it is a free app that stores documents, audio files, and videos. Therefore, to use CloudOn, it will first ask for your username and password for a cloud-based account. Thus, I recommend to first get the Dropbox app, create an account, and then use CloudOn.

The greatest benefit of using CloudOn is that, with Dropbox, students can start their essays in class by using the CloudOn app. Then, at home, they can obtain their files by opening up their Dropbox account from their home computers. Therefore, we can begin work in class using the iPads and then students can finish it at home on their own, as long as they have a computer, Internet access, and remember their Dropbox username and password. In addition, they can submit their papers by e-mailing the file to me from their Dropbox account. Figure 4.10 shows the Word files in a Dropbox account as they appear in the CloudOn app. These files, once tapped, can be opened and edited.

If CloudOn is not to your liking, an alternative that you could use in your classroom is an app called Pages. Although pricey, Pages is an app that students can use. Out of all the word-processing apps I have used, it is the most reliable one. My college prep students first used it when writing their research paper. They were able to add photos, videos, charts, diagrams, and other tools to create a 21st-century research essay. Pages allows users to upload different photos and videos, which CloudOn does not allow users to do from an iPad.

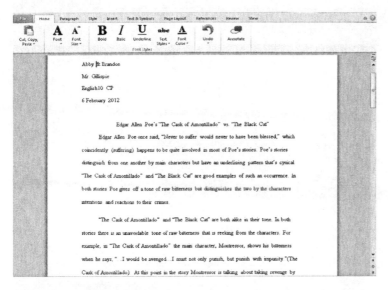

FIGURE 4.9 CloudOn Word file

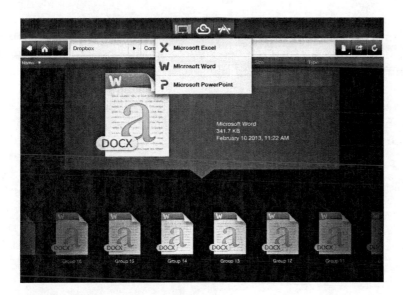

FIGURE 4.10 CloudOn Dropbox files

When I first introduced Pages to my students, they had a difficult time adjusting to the app as is it a bit different from Microsoft Word; the first day we used it, students had trouble figuring out how format a document to double space and create a header. To make this easier, I spent half a class period first teaching students how to format a paper in MLA format using the Pages app. We covered how to double space, add a header, adjust the margins, and add media. From there, students were able to complete the assignment on their own.

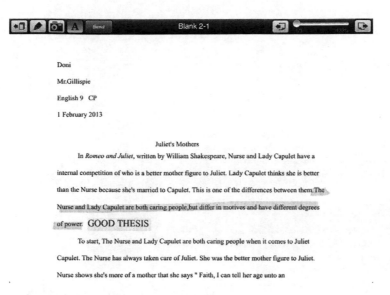

FIGURE 4.11 Grading a paper with Type on PDF

The great aspect of Pages is, once a user begins typing a document, he or she has an option to e-mail the document as a Pages file, a PDF, or a Microsoft Word document. Thus, if students begin a document in class and then want to finish it at home, they can e-mail their file as a Word document. Furthermore, if I want to collect their papers electronically, I can have students send their final drafts as a PDF. From there, I can open it up in a PDF annotation app (such as Type on PDF) and write my comments on the essay with a marker (Figure 4.11). Once I make my comments, I can e-mail it back to the student to see.

Skitch

Standard: 10.L.3

Write and edit work so that it conforms to the guidelines in a style manual (MLA Handbook).

Task: Formatting a paper in MLA

Tools: Skitch

Skitch is another app that can be used to teach MLA format. With Skitch, I have students annotate images that are in the iPad's Camera Roll.

I have been able to use Skitch in two ways. First, when reviewing letter-writing, I have created an incorrectly formatted business letter and uploaded it

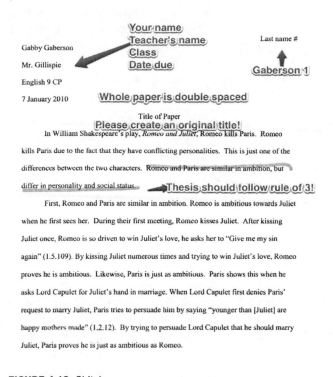

FIGURE 4.12 Skitch

to Schoology. From there, students open it with Skitch, and annotate the letter, highlighting exactly what is wrong. It's an easy way to assess whether or not students understand how to format a business letter properly.

In a similar fashion, I also have taught with Sktich. I have used the app to annotate a sample paper and how to correctly format it in MLA format (Figure 4.12). After teaching students how to effectively format a paper in MLA, I asked them to find a paper from Google Images that was incorrectly headed. From there, they saved the picture to the iPad's Camera Roll, opened the picture in Skitch, and annotated the document, identifying the errors in formatting.

Explain a Website and Flashcardlet

Standard: 10.W.8

Gather relevant information from multiple authoritative and digital sources, avoiding plagiarism, and following a standard format for citation.

Task: Finding and citing reliable sources

Tools: Explain a Website, Flashcardlet

One of my favorite aspects of the Common Core Standards is that students will have to complete short research projects. Thus, it is important to find tools and apps to help them with their research and writing a research paper.

One of the ways in which I teach my students how to follow the research process is by writing a culminating research essay at the end of the year. Transforming the research paper with the iPad was difficult. There are not many apps available to update the process. In fact, I bet whoever comes up with user-friendly apps to help teachers and students with the research paper will make a lot of money.

I did the best I could with what I could find. Before the iPads, I taught the research paper in a traditional way; students brought in index cards, they wrote source cards and note cards, arranged them when writing their outlines, and then wrote rough drafts and final drafts.

It only made sense that I would try to update these steps and use the iPads to do so. I first started by transforming the way in which students demonstrated their knowledge of reliable resources. After discussing what constitutes a reliable source, I asked students to find a reliable Internet source on the Web. Then, using the Explain a Website app, students found a reliable website and created a video recording discussing the different elements of the website that made it reliable. Users of the app can use a pen or highlighter as they record their video (Figure 4.13). They then exported their videos to the iPad's Camera Roll and uploaded these videos to our Schoology course (Figure 4.14). I then viewed them to see who understood exactly what criteria are needed for a source to be reliable. It is definitely worth the money.

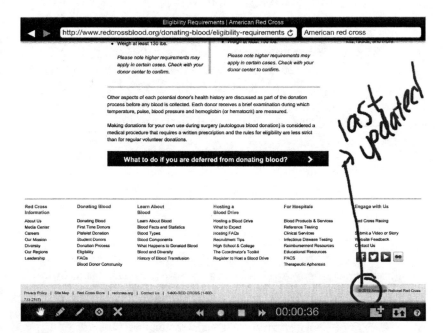

FIGURE 4.13 Explain a Website

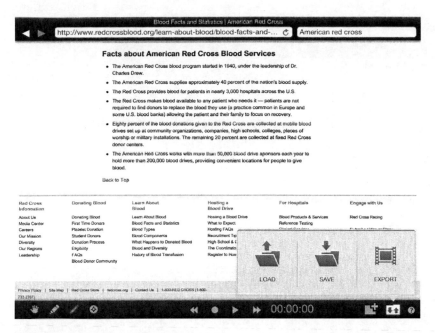

FIGURE 4.14 Explain a Website

I then asked students to organize their research with source cards and note cards. My colleague, Ashlin Henderson, found and shared an app called Flashcardlet. With this app, students can create flash cards. The app's primary focus is for vocabulary review, but my students tried to use it to create source cards and note cards for research.

When you open the app, you can create your own deck of cards. I had students name their decks with their own name. From there, they could write a card; the top card was the front of an index card, and the bottom card was the back. I had students create their source card (in MLA format) on the top, and put a fact from that source on the bottom. This way, they could keep track of the source the information came from, as it was on the top card (Figure 4.15).

For each new fact, students could easily copy and paste the information from the source card onto the top of the next card. In addition, students could copy and paste lines from sources from the Internet into Flashcardlet; all they needed to do afterwards to cite correctly was put quotation marks around the fact and put the citation at the end. At the end of the process, they could e-mail their cards to me so I could grade them.

While it was an updated way to conduct research, there are some annoying aspects to the app. First, users cannot underline or italicize titles, so titles of newspapers and books were not correctly cited in MLA. In addition, when students e-mail their cards to themselves, they could not work with them from home; they needed to use the app to update and work on their cards. Therefore, students could research from home, but they could not continue writing their source cards and note cards until the next class period. Fortunately, this will not

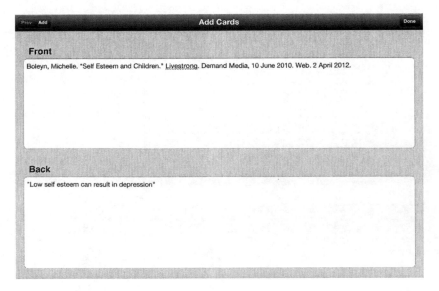

FIGURE 4.15 Flashcardlet

be an issue when our school goes 1:1, and students can take their iPads home with them.

The app does, however, help students organize their research; in the past, I have had trouble with students losing their actual index cards. Students would be frustrated because they lost their research, and I easily became frustrated with them. With the Flashcards app, there was no chance of losing their cards, as they stayed right there on the iPad. The app also makes it easier to write down information, as students can copy and paste information from the Internet instead of writing it down. However, this was all students wanted to do; they did not want to paraphrase information, they wanted to copy and paste all the information from the Web.

Creating a Research Website with Weebly

Standard: 10.W.7

Conduct short as well as more sustained research projects to answer a question or solve a problem, narrow or broaden inquiry when appropriate, and synthesize multiple sources on the subject, demonstrating understanding of the subject under investigation.

Task: Writing a research paper

Tools: Pages, Weebly

For the actual crafting of the research paper, I had students use Pages to write their outlines and rough drafts. This way, they could work on them in class and e-mail their drafts to themselves as a Word file to work on at home. While this was not exactly the most revolutionary way to write the research paper, it at least utilized the tools on the iPad and helped students with the process. From there, we wrote final drafts in class with Pages.

One of the greatest perks of using Pages is that the app allows users to upload photos and videos from the iPad's Camera Roll and import them into a document. Thus, for the first time, I allowed students to add multimedia to their research papers. They were able to add photos and videos to their research papers under two conditions. First, they had to create these products themselves; I did not want students to just take videos from YouTube or photos from the Web. I wanted the entire research paper to be a product in which every aspect was created by the student. As a result, they created essays in which they added videos of themselves reading the paper and pictures to sustain reader interest.

While my college prep students wrote a research paper filled with pictures, videos, and diagrams with the Pages app, I gave my general-level students a different assignment to differentiate. Rather than write a research paper, I had them create a research-based website with the information they found. Like my college prep students, my general-level class conducted research, created source cards and note cards with Flashcardlet, and wrote an outline and rough draft on Pages. Rather than write a research paper, I had them create a final draft of their paper by creating a website using Weebly. Students could add video, audio, and other files. I first had students type paragraphs in Pages; they wrote an introduction with thesis, three body paragraphs with citations, and a conclusion. From there, they edited/revised their drafts and copied the text into their Weebly websites (Figure 4.16).

FIGURE 4.16 Weebly

After students wrote and revised their rough drafts, they then pasted each paragraph as an individual page on their website. Students had a total of six web pages on their websites: a home page (their introduction), three body paragraphs (each their own page), a conclusion page, and a "Works Cited" page. They also added polls, YouTube videos and pictures (they had to cite them as well).

My students preferred making the website to writing an actual paper. They enjoyed creating an authentic product as opposed to typing a paper. This assignment also held more relevance to them; many students told me that creating a website is a skill that would hold value to them in the future. Furthermore, many students were surprised to find out that you could create a website on the Web without the need to learn HTML. It's important to note that students can add text into their websites on the iPad. However, users can't add video, document, or audio files into their websites from the iPad. They can do so from a desktop computer. Thus, we had to create our websites in the computer lab. Hopefully, these features will change in the future.

Grading Essays and Student Work

Grading any type of essay on the computer or iPad is a different process and, if you are not organized, it can be an overwhelming experience. With work that could not be printed out because it was either published or turned in online, such as Storybird, I primarily made my comments on the rubrics I used to assess students. This was a dramatic change for me, as I am used to the actual task of writing comments on my students' actual written work.

There are ways in which you can mark on student papers on the iPad. As stated before, if your students use the Pages app, they can e-mail the document to you as a PDF. From there, once you open it up in your e-mail, you can annotate it with a PDF annotation app such as Type on PDF. From there, once you make your comments, you can e-mail it back to that student to see.

Despite these options, I still prefer to grade on a paper that is printed out and I can have in my hands. I find that students get the best feedback from me if I actually underline problem areas and address how to change it. Therefore, when possible, I still ask students to print them out for me to grade. It is simply what works for me and how I can give the best and most effective feedback to my students. My advice is to try out new ways of having students turn in essays and see which method of grading works best for you and your students.

In terms of how I changed the development of my rubrics, I create rubrics in a similar fashion to the way I created them before the iPads arrived. For various essays, such as the research paper and the Storybird narrative, I add a multimedia grade that accounts for 10% of their final grade. This ensures students' pictures or videos enhance the overall work. For the narrative, this simply entails that students added pictures that related to the text/content they had written. For the research paper, 10% of the grade related to whether videos, audio files, and pictures enhanced the overall product and related to the content on the page.

I made this minor change primarily because I wanted to address creativity skills yet still keep the assignment focused on Common Core Standards. Thus, this minor change in my rubrics ensured that the other 90% of my grading would still assess students' writing abilities and not their use of technology. As a result, students spent more time on writing a well-crafted essay and did not spend a lot of time on the multimedia aspect, as it was only 10% of their grade. This keeps the focus of all writing assignments on the Common Core Standards.

Writing Poetry with iTellaStory and Songify

Standard: 10.L.5

Demonstrate an understanding of figurative language, word relationships, and nuances in word meanings.

Task: Writing poems

Tools: iTellaStory, Songify, AutoRap

Whenever I bring up the subject of poetry during public speaking engagements, I usually express my disdain for teaching it. I find the entire process painful; students struggle to analyze it, and with the exception of a few students, they can't write it well. It can be a painful process.

However, the iPad has honestly changed my perspective on poetry. I have found a few apps that make poetry-writing a fun, interesting, and, at times, hilarious process. I first found the app iTellaStory when teaching the Romantic period in American literature. While reading Whitman, Dickinson, and Poe, I wanted students to write a poem that reflected the content and style of Romantic poets.

That's where iTellaStory comes in. This app is a neat way to create 21st-century poems. With iTellaStory, students can record their voices and add different nature sounds in a second layer of audio. Figure 4.17 shows the screen in which students create their recordings. They can also select a picture to display on the iPad as the recording plays.

Then, after reading the Romantic poets and analyzing the Romantic qualities in those poems, I had students find a nature image in Google Images one day. From there, I gave them their assignment: write a Romantic poem about that image. I wanted their poems to mirror the style and content of many Romantic writers. They primarily had to write about an element of nature that led them to some insight or epiphany.

Students came in the next day with their poems, and many were embarrassed about what they wrote. I then gave them the period to bring the Romantic era of literature into the 21st century; they had to record their poem, add nature sounds, and then e-mail them to me to listen to and assess.

At first, students were reluctant; they tend to dislike any activity that requires them to record and listen to their voices. However, as they added nature sounds

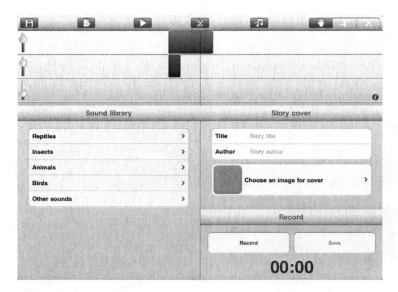

FIGURE 4.17 iTellaStory

such as thunder, reptiles, insects, animals, birds, and other sounds, they relaxed and started to enjoy the process. By the end of the period, students' attitudes about their poetry-writing completely changed, and they wanted to share their recordings. This reversal in reaction to their poems helped me reach an epiphany about teaching: I realized that, perhaps, if I find new and exciting ways to teach a concept, it can be an enjoyable and exciting process for everyone.

Other apps that can be used with poetry-writing are Songify and AutoRap. These are, without a doubt, the best apps I have found to date. Both allow users to record their voice, select a beat, and turn what they say into an actual song (Figure 4.18). If you are somebody who likes laughing and learning to occur in your classroom, I guarantee you that Songify or AutoRap will do the job.

When I first found out about these apps at a conference, I immediately wanted to use them in the classroom. The day I introduced AutoRap is one of those experiences I will always remember; students laughed as they recorded and changed the beats to their songs. They left my classroom with smiles on their faces. I guarantee that it will make for a memorable experience in your classroom.

You can use these apps in a few ways. I first had students use them during a lesson on figurative language. After reviewing the different types of figurative language that authors can use in their writing, students can create a song with as many examples of figurative language as possible. From there, students began thinking of different examples, wrote down their lyrics, and then recorded their songs.

Some students were a bit fearful of the app when I first introduced it, as they were afraid that they would actually have to sing. However, after they realized that their spoken words would be modified and their voice would be completely unrecognizable, they relaxed quite a bit. Once they created their songs, they e-mailed them to me.

FIGURE 4.18 Songify

You can also have students use them to regurgitate their notes; this musical method may help them to retain information from a lecture, as they can memorize the notes as songs. You can have students create songs with a specific amount of syllables or rhyme scheme and record them with Songify or AutoRap. While teaching Shakespeare, you can have students write sonnets and record them with the apps. Seeing as how many songs and lyrics are poetic, I see the app quite fitting with the recording of poetry. In addition, students can e-mail their songs directly to you, as long as their iPad has an e-mail account tied to it. This makes the products students create with the app easier to access and assess.

The only problem I have encountered with these assignments is that some students do not speak directly into the iPad's microphone, so it can be difficult to understand their lyrics. If you plan on grading their songs, I suggest asking students for a copy of their lyrics to read as you listen to their song. This way, you can follow the lyrics as you listen to their songs.

Gabit, the Camera Roll, and Animoto

Standard: 10.RL.3

Analyze how complex characters develop over the course of a text.

Task: Writing poems

Tools: Gabit, Camera Roll, Animoto

FIGURE 4.19 Gabit

I have also asked students to use different apps to record their poems to show their knowledge about novels and other reading selections. I asked my sophomore students to write a "Who Am I?" poem in the voice of a character from *Romeo and Juliet*. They wrote out their poems for homework. They then used the Gabit app to create a cartoon version of the character (Figure 4.19). From there, they recorded their poem and uploaded the recording of the character reciting the poem to Schoology. Once they uploaded, students watched one another's recordings to guess which character the poem described.

I also asked my sophomores to complete a similar assignment while reading *The Crucible*. However, instead of using Gabit, which is a bit juvenile, I asked students to act as the character while reading the poem with the iPad's Camera Roll. From there, they uploaded their videos and typed their poems to Schoology for others to watch and for me to grade.

Yet another way in which you can incorporate poetry is through transforming poems into music videos. I asked my freshmen to write a biopoem for homework. Their biopoem had to be in the voice of a character from *To Kill a Mockingbird*. From there, they then used the Animoto app to type their poem, add music, and add a background to create a music video about the character. By the time they finished, they had created a video poem filled with pictures, text, music, and a background (Figure 4.20). From there, they downloaded their video to the Camera Roll, and then uploaded their videos to our Schoology course for others to view and for me to grade.

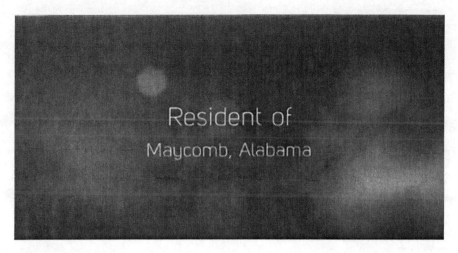

FIGURE 4.20 Animoto

Diaries and Note-taking with Evernote

Standard: 10.RL.2

Summarize the key supporting details and ideas of a text.

Task: Diaries and note-taking

Tool: Evernote

When reading Homer's *The Odyssey*, I wanted my students to understand Odysseus' long journey and his ability to mentally persevere as he tried to find his way home. Thus, for each of the books of *The Odyssey* we read, I asked students to write letters to Penelope in the voice of Odysseus explaining his different encounters during his journey.

To do so, I asked my students to use the Evernote app to create these diaries. Students can write daily entries by opening up the app and logging in (Figure 4.21). They can also add audio files and photos to their journals. In addition, students can share their journals with whoever they choose; all they have to do is opt to share a folder, type in that person's Evernote e-mail, and past and future posts will sync directly to that account. Thus, students share their folders with me via e-mail, and I can access all students' diaries as they write them throughout the unit (Figure 4.22).

The Evernote app can also work for basic note taking as well. If you want students to write class notes using the iPad, you can have your students use Evernote. They can write notes. If a student is absent, he or she can obtain

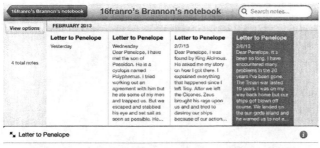

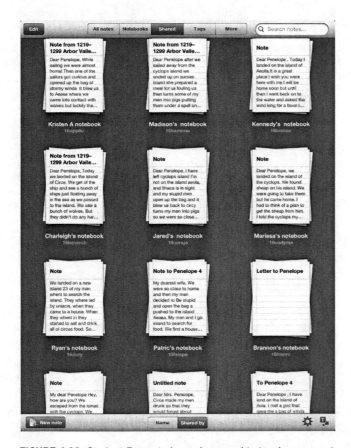

Dear Penelope,

It's been so long. I have encountered many problems in the 20 years I've been gone. The Trojan war lasted 10 years. I was on my way back home but our ships got blown off course. We landed on the sun gods island and he warned us to not eat his cattle but my men ate the cattle still and they're dead now. I left the island but I have something to tell you and I feel awful about it. I cheated on you. I don't even know how. Calypso seduced me somehow every night for 7 years and kept me on her island like a slave. I have cried many days because I longed to be back in Ithaca and be with you and my son, Telemachus. Then one day, Hermes showed up with a message from Zues saying to let me go but before I left, calypso gave me a raft and some provisions. When I set sail, Poseidon destroyed my raft and I washed up on the island Scheria. I hid in a pile of leaves and fell into a deep sleep. This was my only chance to write you during this time I've been away. Hopefully I'll be home soon but until then, just know that I love you.

Your love,
Odysseus

FIGURE 4.21 *The Odyssey* Evernote diary

FIGURE 4.22 Student Evernote journals synced to teacher account

the class notes by asking a student to share his or her Evernote files, as students can e-mail them to one another. This ensures that everybody is obtaining course notes.

Conclusion

Overall, technology has completely transformed the way students write in my classroom. With narrative-writing, students are published authors of narratives, thanks to Storybird. Each student is able to write essays with Microsoft Word due to CloudOn.

While I still have a long way to go when it comes to transforming the way my students conduct research, there are tools available to help students create a multimedia website and essay. The iPad has also helped students to create hilarious poems and paperless notes. All in all, the iPad has helped to make the writing process more engaging, interactive, and meaningful to my students. While my students are writing more, many of the same problems with capitalization, grammar, and spelling still exist. However, many of my students, regardless of ability level, find the writing process more relevant and exciting than in previous years.

Transforming the way my students write in my classroom has been, without a doubt, one of the most satisfying experiences I have had teaching. By publishing their own work, students see the value and purpose of writing; they understand that writing is meant to be shared with the world, not just read by the classroom teacher. As a result, my students of all levels and abilities enjoy writing more than in past years.

5

Transforming Reading with iPads

The first day we used the iPads for academic purposes was a day I will never forget. I remember it just like yesterday; we were in the midst of reading Arthur Miller's *The Crucible*. Students had to bring their textbooks to class every day in order to read the play as a class.

Students hated their textbook, and I could not blame them. Our textbooks are about 8 pounds and are extremely taxing on the back of anyone who carries one. Students longed for days in which they did not need to bring them to class; they would continually ask me each day if they needed to bring their textbooks. Some did not even bother bringing them at all.

So when the iPads finally arrived, they actually gave a round of applause when I told them they could leave their textbooks at home for the rest of the school year. Our textbook company offers online text accessibility as a companion to our textbook. I set up an account at my.hrw.com, provided a generic username and password on the board, and students logged in with that password each and every day. I have the option to give each student his or her own username and password, but they can all log in at the same time with the same login information. So, if you have this option, just create one student account and have students use that. It will save you time.

My very first lesson with the iPads was not exactly the most creative; we needed to get through the end of Act II of the play, so we just transferred our focus from reading out of the textbook to reading from the iPads. I am not exaggerating when I say that students were more engaged by simply switching from our textbooks to the iPads; one student even stated how cool the simple act of reading had become just by reading and finger-swiping pages from our iPads.

I am still amazed by the reaction. I initially laughed at this reaction; my lesson was the exact same as the previous day. The only difference was the iPads. But this simple change excited students and made reading more enjoyable. If I had known this was all it would take to excite my students, I would have bought 30 iPads years ago with my own money. Needless to say, the online text accessibility is a great feature; to this day, students love it and have not given a second thought to their gargantuan textbooks.

This is just one of the ways the iPad has changed reading instruction in my classroom. With the plethora of apps and Web tools on the iPad, there are many different ways in which you can transform the way in which you transform reading instruction and activities in which students demonstrate knowledge of what they have read. Many of the ideas highlighted can be used even if you do not teach the same texts as I do; many of the lessons focus on skills that can be taught in almost all literary texts.

Anticipation Guides with Poll Everywhere

Standard: 10.RL.2

Determine a theme or a central idea of a text and analyze its development.

Task: Anticipation guide

Tool: Poll Everywhere

Some of the best discussions I have ever had with my students have been through the use of anticipation guides. These are commonly used by many teachers in my school. In the past, when preparing to read a novel, I would pass out a handout with 10 different opinion-based statements with which students will either agree or disagree. These statements refer to particular themes that will be seen in the upcoming text for students to keep in mind. Thus, this assignment can help students understand themes and how they develop throughout the course of a text. From there, we would hold debate-based conversations, and students would support their viewpoints over each statement with logic and reasoning.

To make this paperless, I use Poll Everywhere. With it, I can create up to 10 free polls with an account. Thus, I create a separate poll for each question on polleverywhere.com and project each one at a time. Once it is projected, students go to pollev.com and type in the numeric code that corresponds to whether they agree or another code if they disagree. The results then appear live on the projector as students submit their responses (Figure 5.1). From there, I will ask particular students what they thought and ask them to explain their reasoning.

Students enjoy this anticipation guide, and it is more interactive than ever before. As we hold discussions, I encourage students to re-enter the code if a student's comment has changed their opinion. Therefore, as we hold discussions, the poll will change up until it has reached its maximum number of 30 votes per poll. If I want to use the poll again in another class, I simply clear the data to reset the data back to zero votes.

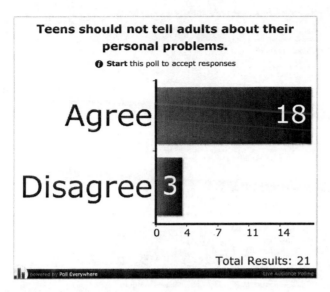

FIGURE 5.1 Poll Everywhere

Annotating Texts with Webnotes and iBooks

Standard: 10.RL.10

Read and comprehend literature.

Task: Annotating texts

Tools: Webnotes, iBooks

Besides Poll Everywhere and anticipation guides, I always try to have students interact with their texts; I ask them to summarize, identify concepts, evaluate a theme, express their opinions, and anything else that makes them underline key parts of a text and write notes as they read. This can help them retain and comprehend more of what they have read. With the textbook, this is difficult to do; they simply can't write in their textbooks. They have to turn it in at the end of the year.

As a result, I would give students a chart. On the left, they would write down a line from the text they were reading. On the right, they would write down a question, comment, connection, or evaluation of that line. This is not exactly the easiest way to annotate a text; it takes far too long for students to switch between the text and a handout. The best way to annotate is for it to be a natural part of the reading process and to truly interact with the text as they read.

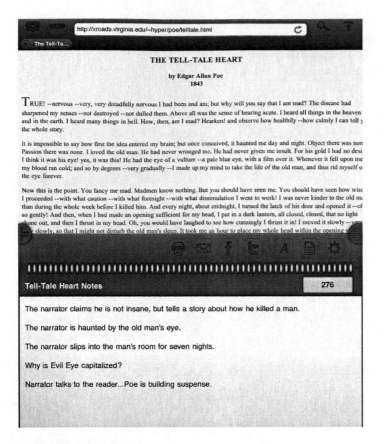

FIGURE 5.2 Webnotes

An app I like and that my students have had success in annotating with is a free app called Webnotes. Webnotes allows for a split-screen effect. On the top or left side of the screen, students can follow the online textbook or any website they are reading. On the bottom or right side, they can write notes about that textbook or website. This is a great way for students to annotate and interact with a text as they read (Figure 5.2).

Apple has an app called iBooks and a wide selection of books in its iBookstore. One of the great features of iBooks is that students can write virtual notes. In addition, teaching American literature and other classic novels has one bonus: many of the texts are in the public domain and are *free* in Apple's Bookstore. I do not use iBooks that often due to the fact that students do not take their iPads home, so we stick with actual novels. However, students who bring their own iPads to class can access many class novels in the iBookstore for free. When our school goes 1:1 with iPads, I will definitely switch from using hardcover books to iBooks.

iBooks has a great definition feature; if a user taps and holds a certain word, it has a "define" option. This can help struggling students, especially when we read higher-level texts such as *The Adventures of Huckleberry Finn* or *The Scarlet*

Letter. In addition, students can create Post-its and place them on individual pages; they can type in comments. This acts as a 21st-century manner of annotating. While I wish the annotations would appear on the text, they are highlighted and students can refer back to them when they click the tab on which they posted.

Visiting Websites with RedLaser

Standard: 10.RIT.1.6.8

Reading informational texts.

Task: Visiting online informational texts to read and discuss

Tool: RedLaser

RedLaser makes visiting websites efficient and easy. RedLaser is an app in which a user can scan QR codes. These QR codes take whoever scans it to a website.

RedLaser also helps students who like to move around to get out of their seats. For lessons in which I want all students to visit a website, such as reading informational texts online, I create a QR code at createqrcode.appspot.com. I then copy and paste the website we will travel to into the box, and then click "Create QR code." It then gives a QR code (similar to the ones you see in magazines, newspapers, and on television) that students scan and open with the RedLaser app (Figure 5.3).

Create QR Code

Google Chart API URL

http://chart.apis.google.com/chart?cht=qr&chs=300x300&chl=http%3A//my.hrw.com/&chld=H|0

Created by Paxmodept

FIGURE 5.3 createqrcode.appspot.com

Students usually have to get up out of their seat to scan the QR code, as they must be aligned with the whiteboard. Students usually enjoy getting up to scan the board; it gets them moving out of their seat for a short amount of time. After about a minute of scanning the board to make sure everyone is on the same page, we can begin the lesson or activity. This simple task is much easier than asking 30 students to type in the same 30-character URL in the Safari Web browser.

Understanding Historical Context with Safari and Keynote

Standard: 10.RIT.10

Read and comprehend literary nonfiction.

Task: Visit and read informational websites to understand the historical context surrounding a text

Tools: Safari, Keynote

One of the most important aspects of teaching literature is teaching historical context surrounding a text. This can help students develop an understanding of the time period and a deeper understanding of other literary standards. When we discuss the time period surrounding a novel, I always tell my students that, while I can give them a general awareness of the time period, I am by no means a history expert. Luckily, the iPad has helped my students and me as we try to understand certain time periods.

Before reading novels such as *Of Mice and Men*, *The Great Gatsby*, *To Kill a Mockingbird*, and more, I put students into groups and gave them one aspect

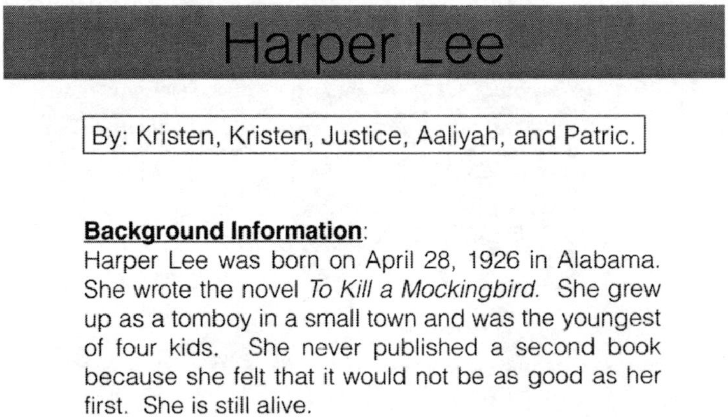

Harper Lee

By: Kristen, Kristen, Justice, Aaliyah, and Patric.

Background Information:
Harper Lee was born on April 28, 1926 in Alabama. She wrote the novel *To Kill a Mockingbird*. She grew up as a tomboy in a small town and was the youngest of four kids. She never published a second book because she felt that it would not be as good as her first. She is still alive.

FIGURE 5.4 Keynote

of the time period that they should be familiar with as they read the particular novel. From there, three students researched that topic on the Web using the Safari Web browser. Another student opened Keynote and began preparing a Keynote presentation about their assigned topic. They had about 30 minutes to find information and pictures and type it into a Keynote (an app similar to PowerPoint) presentation. At the end of class, each group projected their Keynote and presented their topic while the rest of the class listened and jotted down notes (Figure 5.4).

Puppet Pals

Standard 10.RL.2

Provide an objective summary of a text.

Various reading literature standards (depending upon what you highlight in a rubric).

Task: Summarize a text

Tool: Puppet Pals, iMovie, News Booth, Intro Designer Lite

While it can be used for digital storytelling and narrative purposes, I used Puppet Pals as a way for students to show their understanding of a text (Figure 5.5). Puppet Pals is a free app in which students can create puppet shows with fairy-tale puppets. These videos can be saved in the app or exported to the iPad's Camera Roll.

FIGURE 5.5 Puppet Pals

I first used the app with my students while reading short stories. I had students get into partners and summarize a story of their choice. We first reviewed summarizing, and from there, students wrote an objective summary on paper. After I approved each pair's summary, they then re-enacted their summary by using the Puppet Pals app. When each group finished, we watched the video summaries as a way of reviewing individual short stories for an upcoming final test. While Puppet Pals is free, the app also has other types of characters and templates that can be downloaded as well. With the talk show template, political figures, and more, Puppet Pals is an app that teachers and students can use in other content areas as well. Figures 5.6–5.8 illustrate different themes the app offers.

FIGURE 5.6 Puppet Pals templates

FIGURE 5.7 Puppet Pals templates

FIGURE 5.8 Puppet Pals templates

Newscasts with iMovie, Intro Designer, and News Booth

If you want your students to illustrate their understanding of a text in a more sophisticated manner, iMovie is a great app to do so. It is one of my favorite apps to use that fosters creativity. Students have used iMovie for quite a few assignments to demonstrate their understanding of what they have read. When I am running low on new apps/ideas to use in my classroom, iMovie is my go-to app for creativity.

iMovie allows users to create movies with transitions, music, text boxes, and many other features. While it does take time for students to learn how to use it, it's a fantastic app that truly sparks creative thought in the classroom.

After reading various short stories, I asked my freshman students to script out and film a newscast in which they illustrated major literary elements in an assigned short story. I called this the "Ultimate Guide Newscast." In essence, I wanted students to show their understanding of a specific short story and do so in the style of a newscast (Figure 5.9).

Students first spent a few days scripting out their newscast. From there, they used the iPad's Camera Roll to film and edit their newscast together. Once they filmed all their sequences, they imported their video clips into iMovie and put them in order. Afterwards, they added an introduction to their newscast using the free app Intro Designer Lite (Figure 5.10). With this app, they were able to film an opening to their newscast. They created their opening in the app and then exported the video to the Camera Roll to then import into iMovie. They added music to their opening using iMovie's selection of music.

Students were also able to have a viewer call into their news show using the News Booth app. With this app, students could type in text and place a photo in their news show. From there, they were able to give the effect of someone calling in to give a news report (Figure 5.11). The image was then sent to the Camera Roll. From there, they could import the image into the iMovie project and add a voiceover to the photo.

All in all, this project allowed students to show their knowledge of a short story in a way that was not possible without the iPad. This assignment also shows that it is important to inform students that apps can be used together to create a final product that can look and sound quite authentic.

FIGURE 5.9 Ultimate Guide Newscast

FIGURE 5.10 Intro Designer Lite

FIGURE 5.11 News Booth

iMovie, Animoto, and Music Videos

Standard: 10.RL.3

Analyze complex characters and how they develop over the course of a text.

Task: Create a music video about a character

Tool: iMovie, Animoto

I have also used iMovie to gage whether or not students understood the characters in F. Scott Fitzgerald's *The Great Gatsby*. I called this the "iMovie Character Music Video Assignment." After reading the first few chapters, I asked students to identify traits of a pre-assigned character from the novel. They found pictures from Google, imported them into an iMovie project, and then added music and text to their photos to create a music video about a certain character. Students then exported their movies to the Camera Roll and uploaded them to our Schoology course page.

All in all, the products my students have made with iMovie not only look professional, but in the case of this assignment, they clearly allowed me to see whether or not they understood characters in the text in a completely new way. The different lessons and activities you can plan with iMovie definitely warrants its purchase as it comes preloaded with trailer templates, theme music, and transitions, and users can also import iTunes audio files.

If you do not have the money to spend on an app to create music videos, there is a free alternative. Animoto is a fantastic app to create music videos with

FIGURE 5.12 Animoto

your own videos and photos. The videos, text, and pictures a user imports into the app float in the background as they make their way to the front of the iPad screen. In its free version, users can create a 30-second clip filled with pre-designated music. All you have to do is pick your music and background from the Animoto library, type text, and upload your pictures and videos.

I also used the app as an icebreaker on the first day of school. I asked students, on the first day of class, for them to log in to Animoto and create a 30-second "About Me" music video that would encapsulate who they are as a person. This activity served as both an icebreaker and a way for everyone to get to know one another in a different and innovative way. Figure 5.12 is a screenshot of a student product in which he introduced himself to the class with the app.

Students have also used the app to create summaries over reading selections. They have incorporated different still images along with text to create a 30-second video of a chapter of *To Kill a Mockingbird*. The videos look absolutely professional in quality; it is quite amazing that an app can create such a product. The Animoto app allows students to save their creations directly to the iPad's Camera Roll. From there, students can upload their videos to our Schoology course for their classmates to see.

Popplet Mind Maps

Standard 10.RL.2, 9.RL.3

Determine a theme or central idea of a text and analyze its development over the course of the text.

Analyze complex characters and how they develop over the course of a text.

Various reading literature standards (depending on what you highlight in a rubric).

Task: Create a mind map

Tool: Popplet Lite

Popplet Lite is a free app in the App Store in which users can create mind maps. These mind maps can be used for students to organize and separate information into blocks. I decided to use the app for reading instruction as well. I have introduced it when teaching different American short stories centering on the American Dream. After reading short stories from American literature and discussing theme, I had students identify the themes from each short story and explain them using the Popplet Lite app. This gave a visual image and kick-started a discussion about the commonalities among each of the short stories we studied. Students completed their mind maps and then e-mailed them to me as an image.

I also have had students create mind maps to analyze different characters in a text, such as in Homer's *The Odyssey*. They have typed quotes about characters to explain what it reveals about a particular character. Figure 5.13 is an example of a finished student product. It's a great app to isolate certain skills and have students show their knowledge of reading standards. Popplet's features also make it a great tool to use for pre-writing, as it can be used for webbing and organizing ideas.

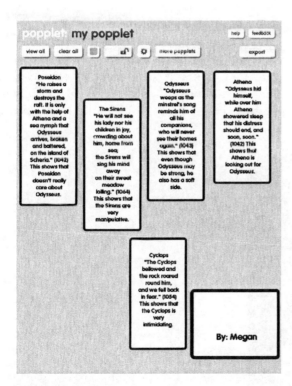

FIGURE 5.13 Popplet Lite

Audioboo Radio Shows and Podcasts

Standard 10.RL.3

Analyze complex characters and how they develop over the course of the text.

Task: Create a radio show

Tool: Audioboo

I also found that scripting and recording radio shows work well with plays. When reading *The Crucible*, I asked my sophomores to record a gossip-style radio show about a particular act in the style of a gossip show broadcast; with a partner, they could use one iPad to record a podcast with the Audioboo app. Audioboo allows users to record their voice for up to three minutes (Figure 5.14). From there, it gives students a link to their audio recording. Therefore, with one iPad, they could record their podcast and on the other, they could record radio sounds to make their radio show sound professional. First, students received a handout that outlined which characters I wanted them to discuss and analyze in their show. From there, students found a partner, and from there, they started scripting their radio broadcast. The next day, students had 20 minutes to record their radio show.

The idea behind the radio show was for students to examine the events of a particular act and character actions in a dramatic fashion. It was an interesting way for students to examine character motivations and summarize plot events in an innovative way. Students recorded their show, published their recordings,

FIGURE 5.14 Audioboo

copied the URL to their recordings, and then posted them to our Schoology course. We then listened to them.

In addition, each quarter, my college prep students must complete an independent reading project. Before the iPads, students had to read a book that was not only grade-level appropriate, but also geared toward their interests. They then, in some manner, had to show me that they understood the novel and analyzed it based on important concepts we learned that quarter. This could be in the form of creating a website, movie, magazine, newspaper, or anything else they could think of.

With the iPads, I decided to change this assignment. While they still had to read a book, I had them complete checkpoints; using our Schoology course, they had to respond to different questions I posted in different Schoology discussion threads.

They had to complete about five different discussion threads while reading their books. At the end of the quarter, they then completed a culminating project; they had to make a podcast using Audioboo.

The end assignment resulted in students recording radio shows; they showed their knowledge of the text using the rubric I gave them. Once they finished their radio show, they had to copy and paste the link to their radio show onto our Schoology page.

Kabaam Comic Summaries and Storyboards

Standard: 10.RL.2

Summarize the key supporting ideas and details of a selection or text.

Task: Create a comic

Tool: Kabaam Comics

During a short story unit, I had students read *Teenage Wasteland* and summarize it for homework; we first discussed the idea of summarizing and taking the main points or ideas from the short story. In class the next day, students then transformed their summaries into a comic version of the short story. Students took pictures of themselves or others (with permission) and added speech bubbles to each picture (Figure 5.15). The frames of their comics had to match each sentence of their summary. From there, they e-mailed their comics to me to grade. This definitely created a more engaging alternative to discussing the short story as a class or completing a worksheet.

Students also used Kabaam while reading *Romeo and Juliet*. After reading the Prologue to Act I of Shakespeare's play, I had students use Kabaam Comics to first translate each of the 14 lines into modern-day English. From there, students found or took pictures, added their translations to each frame, and created a comic

FIGURE 5.15 Kabaam Comics

that summarized the reading selection. Overall, this helped students in their first foray in reading Shakespeare. By first translating the Prologue and then finding or taking pictures that matched their translations, they were able to visualize what they had read, which is an important reading comprehension strategy.

Character Word Clouds with Wordle.net, Tagxedo.com, and Word Foto

Standard: 10.RL.3

Analyze complex characters and how they develop over the course of a text.

Task: Create a word cloud

Tools: wordle.net, tagxedo.com, Word Foto

Students have also created word clouds to show their knowledge of characters or reading selections. A word cloud is an image created solely through the use of words. I have used Word Foto for formative assessments by having students summarize a reading passage and have also had students create word clouds to analyze characters and their traits as well. Figure 5.16 is the Word Foto app in action.

The Web is also filled with an abundance of websites that allow users to create a word cloud on a laptop or desktop computer; wordle.net and tagxedo.com are two great websites to create such clouds. All you have to do is click create, type in words you want, and, from there, the word cloud generates. If a user types in the same word numerous times, that word is displayed more prominently in the photo. You can also pick the shape of your word cloud, the text type and size, color, font, and theme.

These websites do not work on the iPad, but I prefer taking my students to the library to use wordle.net and tagxedo.com on a computer, as the word clouds generated from these sites are of higher quality. Once printed out, they can also be posted to make for a great bulletin board. In addition, Word Foto only allows users to type in around 10 words per file; the amount of words you can type in for one Wordle and Tagxedo file are endless.

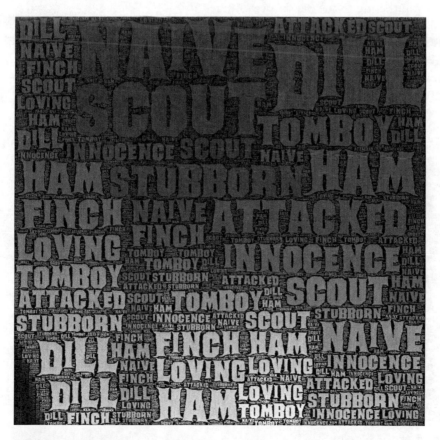

FIGURE 5.16 Word Foto

Assessing Theme and Summarizing with iMovie Trailers

Standard: 10.RL.2

Determine the theme or central idea of a text and analyze its development; compose an objective summary of a text.

Task: Create a trailer to a novel that summarizes and demonstrates awareness of a theme

Tools: iMovie Trailers

Once opened, the iMovie app allows users to create a new project from scratch or to create a trailer like one would see before you watch a movie. I have also had students create trailers in class. Once students open iMovie Trailers, they can choose a trailer template. They must type in text and add photos or videos to their trailer. Once they fill in all the different parts of the template, they will have an authentic trailer set to prearranged music.

After reading *Of Mice and Men*, I asked students to create a trailer to Steinbeck's novella in which they summarized key parts of the text. In addition, I told students that I wanted to be able to view a theme statement in their trailer as well. Students spent one day in class mapping out their trailer and two days creating their trailer in iMovie. In the end, students created sophisticated trailers and were truly engaged while completing the project (Figure 5.17).

FIGURE 5.17 iMovie Trailer

Summarizing with Timeline Builder and Pic Collage

Standard: 9.RL.2

Compose an objective summary of a text.

Task: Create a timeline to create an overview of the events in a text

Tools: Timeline Builder, Pic Collage

Yet another app that students can use to summarize what they have read is Timeline Builder. The app allows students to create a timeline of events filled with pictures to match each event.

While reading *Romeo and Juliet*, my students and I read most of the scenes in class, as Shakespeare's play is quite difficult. With the exception of a few short scenes, I assign different roles to students to read aloud.

One of the problems I encounter is, between reading and completing activities and quizzes, we spend around six weeks reading the play. As a result, when we near the end of the play, students tend to forget what happens at the beginning, as we started it over a month prior.

To combat this problem, the ninth grade English teachers pass out summary sheets for students to complete after we read each scene. Students summarize each scene after they read it. Then, as a way of reviewing for a final test over *Romeo and Juliet*, I have students complete a timeline of the events in the play that they thought led to the title characters' demises. To do so, students use the Timeline Builder app. They use their summary sheet and create a timeline of the most important events that transpire in the play. This is a great way to review all the events of the play, as it forces students to review their summary sheets. It's a great app that can be used to review the events of virtually any text.

If you are looking for a different app for students to use for summarizing purposes, Pic Collage is another tool to assess students' knowledge. I have used it when reading *Of Mice and Men*; after reading each chapter, students wrote a summary of the text. They then took their summary to create their own visual collage. In their collages, they showcased exactly what each chapter was about; they needed to highlight the important aspects of the chapter in terms of plot and character. I usually tell students that they should have at least one image per sentence they write in their original summary. By the time we finished the novella, students had completed six summaries and six collages of what they had read. Figure 5.18 is an example of a collage that summarizes one chapter. Overall, it's a nice way for students to review and demonstrate understanding of what they have read in a visual manner.

A good piece of advice for those who want to use the app with *Of Mice and Men* is that, if you have your students find images with Google Images, tell them that they must be school-appropriate. *Of Mice and Men* is a violent text, as people

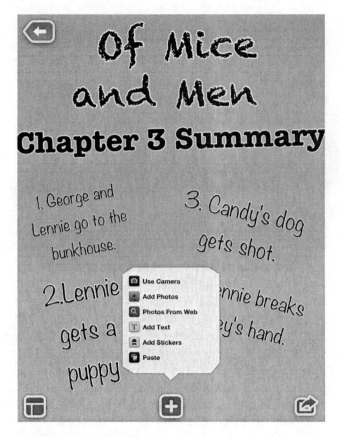

FIGURE 5.18 Pic Collage

and animals die. I did not exactly want my students to look up pictures of dead dogs. Therefore, I told students that they could find a picture of a puppy sleeping to represent this idea in their collage. With this assignment and any other assignment in which students take photos from the Web, it is a good idea to enforce a PG rating on all images.

Figurative Language with Explain Everything

Standard: 9.RL.4

Determine the meaning of words and phrases as they are used in the text, including figurative and connotative meanings.

Task: Create a video explaining figurative language and how it is used in writing

Tools: Explain Everything, ShowMe, ScreenChomp

Figurative language can be tricky for students to remember. There are so many different types and some of the more obscure concepts can be difficult for students to remember. To help, students can show their understanding of figurative language through whiteboard apps. Explain Everything, ShowMe, and ScreenChomp are all whiteboard apps available in the App Store.

I first used these whiteboard apps to replace direct instruction of figurative language. I paired students up and gave them one specific type of figurative language used in literature. From there, students had to research and then create a resource video about an assigned type of figurative language with a whiteboard app (Figures 5.19 and 5.20). To differentiate, I gave low-level students an easier type, such as simile and personification. Advanced students had to create a video about difficult types, such as paradoxes or metaphors. With their partner, students had to create a video on an interactive whiteboard in which they explained the figurative language, gave examples, found an example from a literary text, and then explained how it could be used in narrative-writing. Students shared their videos and then they had to watch one another's videos to obtain notes on the different types of figurative language to ensure that they received information over all types used in literature.

On Fridays, whenever I have about 10–15 minutes left in the class period, I will sometimes have students use a whiteboard app to assess what they learned that week; they create a recording of what they learned and then upload it to Schoology. It's an informal way to reinforce concepts, to have students learn with one another, and to understand which concepts I need to reteach and which students need future interventions.

Onomatopoeia: The use of words whose sounds imitate the sound of the thing being named.

good ex.

Twchhhh brwm brwm brwm bar umm brwm brwm brwm

Sound of an aircraft engine.

Clackity-click/clickity clack – the sound of a train going down the track

FIGURE 5.19 Explain Everything

FIGURE 5.20 Explain Everything

There are so many whiteboard apps available, and if I had to choose my favorite, Explain Everything would be it. It is one of the most unique and useful interactive whiteboard apps. Students can record their voices as they draw with a marker or type with text. The end result is a video that can be uploaded to the iPad's Camera Roll. Many other whiteboard apps do not have this capability.

Teaching Shakespeare with Shakespeare in Bits and Ye Olde English Insults

Standard: 9.RL.2

Read and comprehend literature.

Task: Watch scenes from a cartoon version of *Romeo and Juliet*

Tools: Shakespeare in Bits, Ye Olde English Insults

While still on the topic of *Romeo and Juliet*, one of my favorite apps I have used to teach Shakespeare is definitely Shakespeare in Bits. While it is expensive, I bought it with my iPad and have streamed the content to my students using Apple TV.

I have used Shakespeare in Bits while teaching Romeo and Juliet. While reading the Prologue to each Act, I project the app, we read it together, and from there, we watch the cartoon version that I can play with the app. Figure 5.21 illustrates how the app appeals to visual learners.

It is a fantastic way for students to visualize what they are reading, especially with Shakespeare, which can be extremely difficult for students to comprehend. The lines also come with translations to help the reader.

FIGURE 5.21 Shakespeare in Bits

FIGURE 5.22 Shakespeare in Bits

The app also comes with a character list (with cartoon characters), scene synopses, a place for the reader to write notes, plot summaries, analysis of themes, imagery, information about Shakespeare's life, and so much more (Figure 5.22). The app does have a free version; however, it is limited on features. I have found that by streaming the app's features on my iPad through Apple TV, it can work as a great instructional tool.

If you teach other Shakespeare plays, the company that creates the app does offer other plays as well. You can buy *Macbeth*, *A Midsummer Night's Dream*, *Hamlet*, and *Julius Caesar* in the App Store as well. While I have not used these in my classroom, if they are anything like *Romeo and Juliet*, you and your students will enjoy them.

While I am on the topic of Shakespeare, another fun activity to complete with students is introducing Shakespearean insults. There is even an app to insult others in using language from the Elizabethan era. The app Ye Olde English Insults is a fun app that generates insults for users to speak. We spent the beginning of one period insulting one another before a brief discussion about the insults in the play and how they serve as comic relief and build characterization.

Reading Edgar Allan Poe with iPoe and iPoe 2

> Standard: 10.RL.4
>
> Understand how choices in words and language can influence tone and mood.
>
> Task: Read various short stories by Edgar Allan Poe
>
> Tool: iPoe, iPoe 2

Another app that can be used to help students visualize what they read is iPoe and iPoe 2. Both give users access to interactive versions of various Poe short stories and poems.

The app is, without a doubt, one of the most interactive apps that I know of when it comes to reading. If you turn up the volume, you can hear creepy music as you read. Some pages are dimly lit and you must use light to read certain sections of the page. There are different figures on some pages that you can manipulate as well. Figures 5.23–5.25 show just how innovative the app can be for reading literature.

This has revolutionized the way in which I teach tone and mood. We read certain short stories, such as *The Tell Tale Heart* and *The Masque of Red Death*, as a class, as I project the app from my iPad for students to read. From there, I ask students how they felt as they read the iPoe version of the short story. From there, we come up with a list of words that describe how they felt.

Afterwards, we discuss tone, mood, and the author's attitude/feelings surrounding the text. We discuss tone with relation to both the creators of the

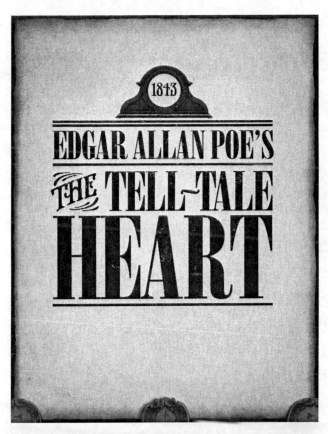

FIGURE 5.23 iPoe

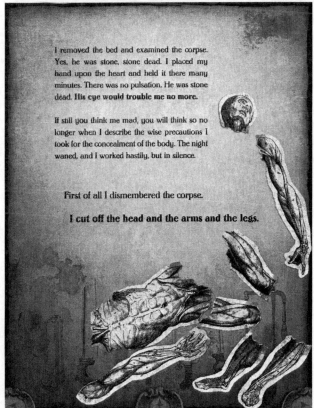

FIGURE 5.24 iPoe

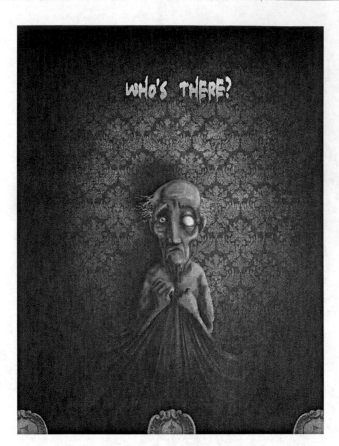

FIGURE 5.25 iPoe

app and Poe's tone. We discuss what the creators of the app have done to create such a unique and scary app and effectually, how it tries to scare the audience. From there, we discuss Poe's short stories and exactly how he creates such an ominous tone in his short stories. Students pinpoint specific language from the short stories to determine Poe's attitude and how he sets the mood in each piece. All in all, the app truly helps in the instruction of these difficult literary techniques.

Conclusion

Over the course of the year, my students have read and demonstrated their understanding of what they have read in a modernized format; as textbooks are being replaced by e-books, it is important for all students to have experience with iBooks and other online textbooks. Students truly prefer this new method of reading; they are stimulated and more engaged by swiping through pages of a book rather than flipping through a bulky textbook. I still test my students over novels to prepare them for standardized tests. However, as they are introduced to new apps and resources to show their comprehension of grade-appropriate texts, they have found reading and discussing more engaging than ever before.

The great aspect of most of the apps and tools highlighted in this chapter is that, with creativity, they can be used for virtually any literary work. Therefore, while I may use many of these apps for texts such as *The Crucible, Of Mice and Men, Romeo and Juliet, To Kill a Mockingbird*, and many others, the same activity can be applied to what you teach, as the activity does not focus on the specific text; it focuses on specific Common Core Standards.

6

Formative Assessment, Summative Assessment, and Gathering Data

An important aspect of teaching is obviously identifying students who are above, at, and below specific standards. Great educators can pinpoint specific students' strengths and areas of weakness and adapt from there. With over 120 students, it can be quite difficult to monitor exactly how many students are above, at, and below each standard with each formative and summative assessment. Teaching both reading and writing, this collection of data can be quite overwhelming at times, as there is so much to teach.

While I definitely prefer other forms of assessment over tests and quizzes, I still use them to help prepare my students for standardized assessments. Moreover, it provides data that can help influence future instruction and understand student learning. Luckily, the iPad and other mobile devices can make this collection of data a bit easier. There are quite a few websites and apps available that help me and can help you easily identify and track who understands class content and who needs more help.

Formative Assessment

Poll Everywhere

I try to formatively assess at the end of each lesson. While some methods of assessing are more data-driven and statistical than others, Poll Everywhere is a fantastic tool to gather data from an entire group of students.

While I have used Poll Everywhere for anticipation guides, it also works easily to formatively assess students. All you need is a desktop computer and students with cell phones or iPads. I go to the website, log in to my account, and create a poll over the indicator I want to assess. This poll can be a multiple-choice question with as many choices as I want, or I can ask open-ended questions where students can type in their answers.

When I use Poll Everywhere to formatively assess, I usually project it on the whiteboard so that students can see the results appear and update live in front

The sycophant went up to the teacher and told him that he was her favorite teacher. Based on the way it is used in the sentence, a sycophant is...

Text a **CODE** to **37607**

Submit a **CODE** to **http://PollEv.com**

A suck-up	**37833**	100%
A fan	**37839**	
A stalker	**37888**	
A nerd	**37925**	

FIGURE 6.1 Poll Everywhere

of them. I tend to create polls in the form of multiple-choice questions, as I have found another website that works better for open-ended, short-answer responses. When I start a poll, students first read the question and try to figure out the answer. From there, they open up pollev.com in Safari on the iPad and type in the code that matches the appropriate response. With the example in Figure 6.1, "suck-up" is the correct answer. Thus, students would type in the number of the corresponding answer in the text box that appears in pollev.com. From there, the results change live on the projector as each student submits a response. They tend to get excited and point out when the poll changes.

As much as I like Poll Everywhere, there are some downfalls to the website when it comes to formative assessment. It is a great tool to collect data as an entire class; however, I can't obtain individual student data with the free version. Although the website allows me to create up to 10 polls with a free account, I can only project one poll at a time for all students to see. Also, when the poll appears and updates, some students may be influenced by the results and submit the response that most students have selected. Therefore, it can skew the data, as some students will select the answers their peers have already submitted.

Overall, the website is a great way to assess a class as a whole. Even if you do not have iPads, it works well because most students have cell phones and can submit their answers via text messaging. If you plan on using Poll Everywhere with iPads or even students' cell phones, I would check with a school administrator before using this website, especially if your school has a policy regarding cell phones in school.

Whenever I talk about Poll Everywhere with teachers at workshops, I am usually asked if I have encountered students typing in inappropriate responses with open-ended questions. Seeing as how the responses are anonymous, it's easy for anyone to type in an inappropriate response and not get caught. While I have not had a problem with this in my classroom, I know other teachers have had this issue. My suggestion is to make clear that the activity is a privilege; if somebody can't handle typing in responses relating to the question at hand, the entire class will have to resort back to pen and paper for our answers. This is my management strategy with any tool; once someone writes or posts something offensive, we do not use the tool anymore.

Socrative

If you want specific student data, socrative.com and the app is a fantastic tool to use in the classroom. I have used Socrative when I needed to obtain all sorts of data. In essence, Socrative is an app and a website that allows teachers to quiz students or obtain feedback after a particular lesson.

In order to implement it in the classroom, I download the Socrative Teacher app on my iPad and students download the Student app on their iPads. Once I open Socrative, the app gives me a room number and the ability to create different types of activities (Figure 6.2). With the Student app, students type in *my* room number and wait for me to begin an activity (Figures 6.3 and 6.4). Thus, the Teacher app is for me to create quizzes and activities, and the Student app is for students to complete them once I activate them.

Socrative has two distinct uses for teachers; the first way in which I use Socrative is through the use of single-question activities (Figure 6.5). Single-question activities are multiple-choice questions, true/false questions, and short-answer responses students can answer at the beginning, throughout, or at the end of a lesson. I can ask a question on the fly either orally or on my projector through a PowerPoint slide. I simply need to activate the multiple-choice,

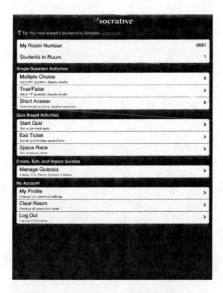

FIGURE 6.2 Socrative Teacher app

FIGURE 6.3 Socrative Student app

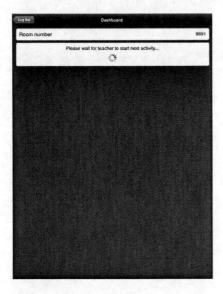

FIGURE 6.4 Socrative Student app

true/false, or short-answer option in my Teacher app, have students open up the Student app and answer the question. The results appear live on my screen as students answer (Figure 6.6). Multiple-choice and true/false questions appear as graphs and short-answer responses appear as students type them.

It is important to note that, with single-question activities, you can't import questions for students to view in the room; you can either give a question orally, or you can make a question slide using a PowerPoint presentation or by writing the questions on the board. Students enter the room I have open on the iPad and answer the single-question activities as I activate them. In addition, I can't

FIGURE 6.5 Socrative single-question activities

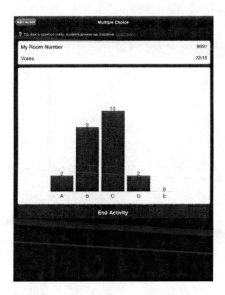

FIGURE 6.6 Socrative multiple-choice question results

obtain specific student names through single-question activities; I only receive answers based on the class as a whole from the bar graph. Thus, I can't tell which students know content and which do not.

If I want specific student data, Socrative has a second category of activities labeled quiz-based activities (Figure 6.7). These activities allow me to run pre-made quizzes that I have previously created under the create, edit, and import quiz function. I prefer these activities for a couple of reasons. First, when I create a quiz and activate it, they can be used to assess individual student data, as the first question of any quiz is "What is your name?" I also like it because I can create questions beforehand that students can answer either at my own or their own pace. Thus, I do not need to ask the questions orally or create PowerPoint slide questions, unlike with the single-question activities. The questions will appear on my students' iPads to answer.

As students complete the pre-made quizzes, I can see how many students have completed the quiz (Figure 6.8). Once the app shows that all students in the room have submitted the quiz, I end the activity and choose the option for Socrative to send an e-mail of the results in a spreadsheet (Figure 6.9).

FIGURE 6.7 Socrative quiz-based activities

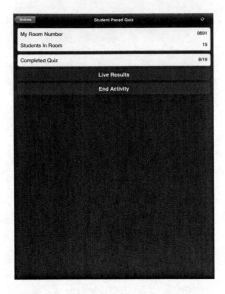

FIGURE 6.8 Socrative Teacher app during quiz

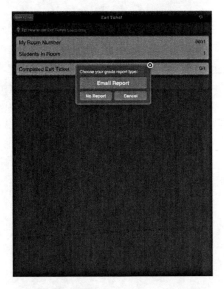

FIGURE 6.9 Socrative quiz report options

The spreadsheet is, without a doubt, the greatest benefit of Socrative; the spreadsheet shows me each student and their answers; questions students got wrong are highlighted in red, and correct answers are highlighted in green. This visual manner makes it easier to see who understands what; if most of a student's responses are primarily highlighted in red, I know that student needs intense remediation. If question one primarily has red responses, I know I need to reteach that specific indicator to the entire class. To sum up, this website makes not only collecting data, but *analyzing* it easier than ever before.

One thing to keep in mind with the pre-made quizzes is that the Socrative Student app informs students whether they got the answer right or wrong right after they answer each individual question. This obviously can be problematic if you plan on using the same quiz in multiple classes, as students can inform the next class about the questions that are on the quiz. If you decide to use Socrative, this is something to keep in mind if you check the correct answers when you develop a quiz.

In addition, it is important to remind students that there is not an option to look back at questions; each question appears one at a time and once a student has answered a question, it is their final answer. This has frustrated students a little; thus, for this reason, I only use Socrative for short quizzes. I find it a bit unfair to give students a test on Socrative when they are unable to review their answers or go back and change them.

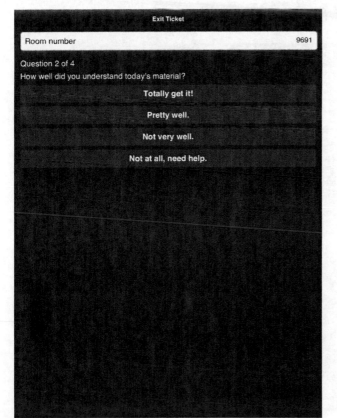

FIGURE 6.10
Socrative exit tickets

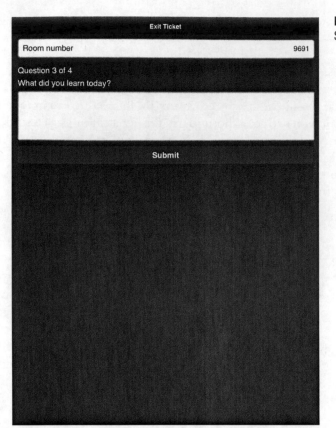

FIGURE 6.11
Socrative exit tickets

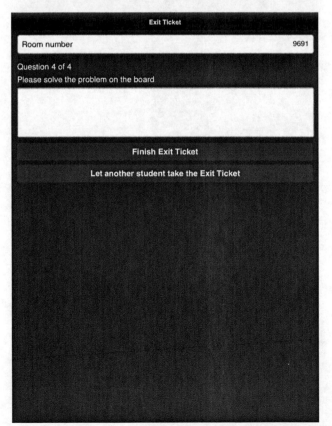

FIGURE 6.12
Socrative exit tickets

Another Socrative quiz–based activity is the use of exit tickets. These types of activities are best suited at the end of a lesson, as they will ask students general questions about a specific lesson. Figures 6.10–6.12 show the types of exit ticket questions that students can answer. There is also an option for a space race in which students can take a quiz as a game; the first student or group to answer all questions wins the game. This can be a great way to review for a final test.

Summative Assessment and Testing

Schoology Tests

When it comes to testing, I prefer to use Schoology tests, as students can review and change answers before they submit them to me. Schoology also has the ability for teachers to create tests and quizzes for students to take in an online format. These tests can contain different types of questions, from multiple-choice, short-answer, and true/false, to ordering, essay, fill-in-the-blank, and matching.

Creating a quiz or test is easy. In fact, if you can create a quiz using Microsoft Word, ExamView, or any other program, you can definitely create a Schoology test. From the add materials option, you click "create test," fill in the test criteria, and start adding questions. Once you are ready to give the quiz, you simply activate it in the "Settings" tab of that quiz.

Students then take the quiz. Taking a quiz is quite simple for students. They open up the iPad, log in to Schoology, find the quiz, and then click "Begin Test/Quiz" (Figure 6.13). From there, the quiz opens, and they answer the questions (Figure 6.14). When they are finished, they click "submit." Results are then recorded.

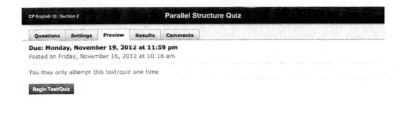

FIGURE 6.13 Beginning a Schoology test

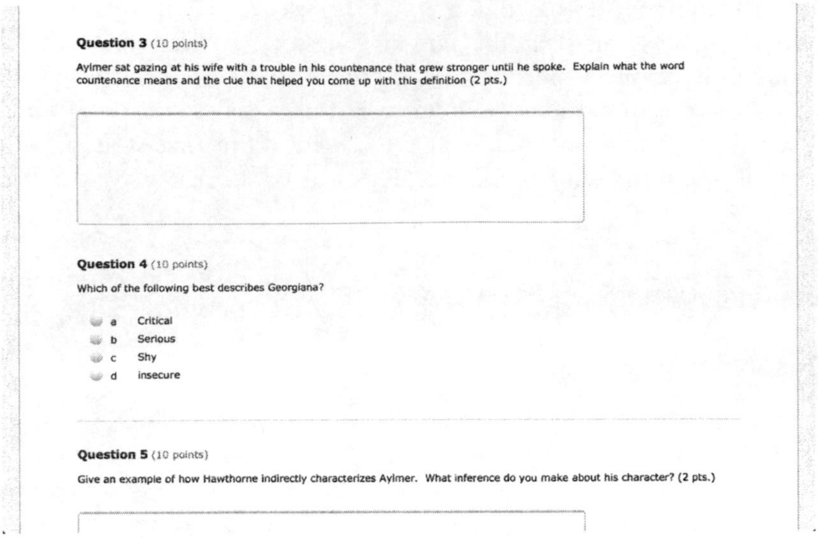

Question 3 (10 points)

Aylmer sat gazing at his wife with a trouble in his countenance that grew stronger until he spoke. Explain what the word countenance means and the clue that helped you come up with this definition (2 pts.)

Question 4 (10 points)

Which of the following best describes Georgiana?

- a Critical
- b Serious
- c Shy
- d insecure

Question 5 (10 points)

Give an example of how Hawthorne indirectly characterizes Aylmer. What inference do you make about his character? (2 pts.)

FIGURE 6.14 Schoology test in progress

Once they finish, an instructor can then see the results in the "results" tab of the test. I can see which students have taken the quiz, how they scored, and exactly how each of my students answered each question and what percentage of students selected each option for multiple-choice tests. Figures 6.15–6.17 show exactly how teachers can view these data. For privacy reasons, student names have been omitted in the screenshots.

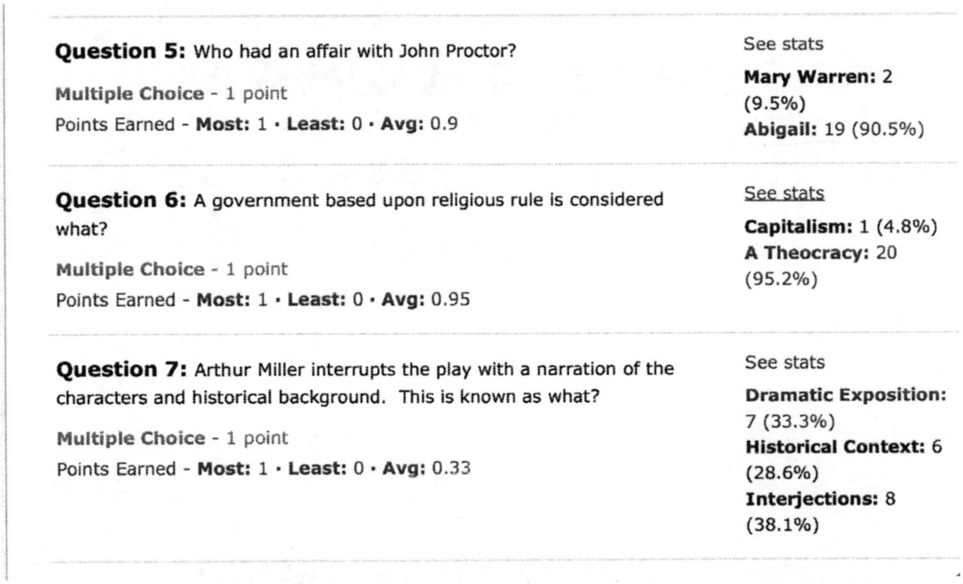

Question 5: Who had an affair with John Proctor?

Multiple Choice - 1 point
Points Earned - **Most:** 1 · **Least:** 0 · **Avg:** 0.9

See stats
Mary Warren: 2 (9.5%)
Abigail: 19 (90.5%)

Question 6: A government based upon religious rule is considered what?

Multiple Choice - 1 point
Points Earned - **Most:** 1 · **Least:** 0 · **Avg:** 0.95

See stats
Capitalism: 1 (4.8%)
A Theocracy: 20 (95.2%)

Question 7: Arthur Miller interrupts the play with a narration of the characters and historical background. This is known as what?

Multiple Choice - 1 point
Points Earned - **Most:** 1 · **Least:** 0 · **Avg:** 0.33

See stats
Dramatic Exposition: 7 (33.3%)
Historical Context: 6 (28.6%)
Interjections: 8 (38.1%)

FIGURE 6.15 Schoology test results and data

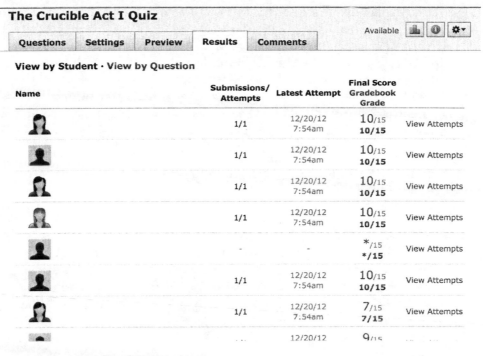

FIGURE 6.16 Schoology test results and data

 **Chelsea**

Submission 1

$0/1$

a. Explanation

b. Dramatic Exposition

c. Historical Context

d. Interjections

Add Comment

FIGURE 6.17 Schoology test results and data

From a teacher's standpoint, the greatest aspect of Schoology tests is that once a student submits his or her test, it is automatically graded, unless, of course, it is a short-answer or essay question. I can pull up the assignment in my iPad, view the grades, and then put them into our school's online grade book. If you opt to use the Schoology grade book, it will even import the grade right into the grade book for you. In addition, the fact that I can also view each student's individual answers also allows me to analyze why a student may have selected an incorrect answer. I no longer have to use Scantron machines to obtain student data.

Reviewing for Tests

Before any test in my class, I typically will hold a review game; the day before the test, we will spend the class period reviewing major concepts they should know. I also use the game as a way to formatively assess whether or not the class is ready for a final test. I have found a few game templates that allow users to create a game show atmosphere in the classroom.

The first website is jeopardylabs.com. I find this website to be quite useful, especially when I have no time to create a review game. When you go to the website, you have two options; you can either create your own *Jeopardy* game, or you can browse through the templates that other users have made (Figure 6.18).

This website makes creating review games much easier than in the past. I also like the scoreboard at the bottom of the screen; it makes tracking each team's progress much easier.

This template can be used in conjunction with the iPads. When we play *Jeopardy*, I assign each group an iPad. From there, teams have one iPad in which they open up a whiteboard app. The App Store is flooded with many different tools that turn the iPad into a whiteboard. From Screen Chomp to Show Me, the iPad allows students to have an interactive whiteboard right in front of them. When a question appears, I give students 10 seconds to write their

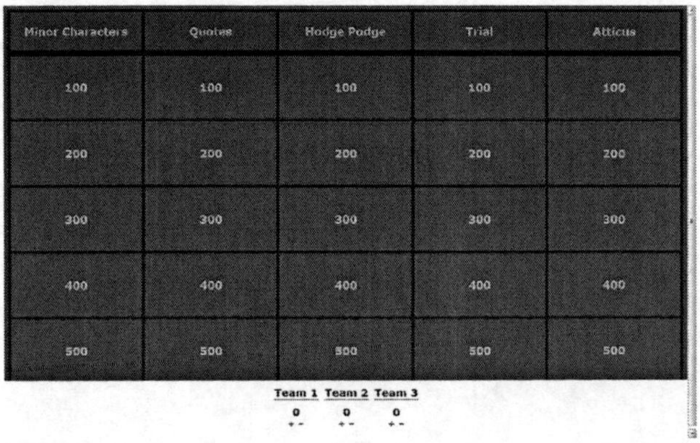

FIGURE 6.18 Jeopardy Labs

response on the iPad. Then, I say "markerboards up," and each team must raise their markerboard to show their answer. I then adjust scores on the *Jeopardy* template as I view their answers.

My main rule with the review game is that students must hold their iPads carefully and raise them up carefully as well. If not, I take away points from the team. When we first played, I had concerns that groups would drop their iPads, as some students can get overwhelmed and raise their iPads up quickly or carelessly. However, I have not encountered this problem.

A simple Google search can also yield some other game templates. The website jc-schools.net/tutorials/ppt-games allows visitors to download templates of different games. I have created review games using *Who Wants to Be a Millionaire?* I usually use this template for whole-class review. I will use the Stick Pick app to randomly call on students for each question. They can select other students as their lifelines. From there, if the whole class answers all questions correctly, I will give each of them one bonus point on the test the next day. The website also has templates for *Password*, *Wheel of Fortune*, and *Are You Smarter than a Fifth Grader?* Overall, it makes review day much easier to plan and more interactive than in the past.

Conclusion

Whether it is a quiz, test, or an end-of-the-period formative assessment, the iPad creates many opportunities to gage student knowledge throughout a unit. While each app or tool has its own quirks and features that make it suitable for one method of assessment in the classroom over another, it's undeniable that my instruction has changed for the better.

Before the iPads arrived, I will admit that I had a difficult time analyzing quiz and test data. In the past, I would simply scan my exams through a Scantron, run an exam analysis at the end, and then review questions that most students missed. However, with Socrative quizzes and Schoology tests, I now have access to a visual representation of not only how many students missed each question, but which students got which questions right or wrong.

This allows me to not only guide those students who need more help, but also refine my future lessons and group students based on their similar strengths and weaknesses. As a result, students have more chances to grasp concepts that they may not have fully understood the first time I taught them. This is because I have a better grasp of each individual student's knowledge of important course concepts.

Communication and Collaboration with the iPad

When I was in middle and high school, I was shy, painfully shy. In fact, I am sure there are quite a few teachers I had that probably wondered if I could even speak.

I rarely said a word in class. Whenever a teacher would call on me, I would always feel my body heat up; my face would turn about 1,000 shades of red. I hated speaking in public. At the time, I could not really pinpoint exactly why. Now that I am older and am able to reflect on the endless amount of embarrassing experiences speaking up in class caused me, I know that I feared being judged. After all, high school is a place in which many fear they are being judged by their peers.

It's pretty ironic that I would go on to teach high school, let alone a public speaking class. I like to think my past experiences give me an empathetic attitude toward my shy students. I try to make my shy students feel safe contributing to class discussions, and I will encourage them to speak up.

I was pleasantly surprised how much the iPad has given these introverted kids a voice; there are so many websites and apps available for students to communicate their thoughts without uttering a single word out of their mouths. I found quickly in the experience that shy students were more comfortable contributing in class chat rooms or discussion threads. I did not anticipate the iPad would give quiet students a way to contribute to discussion; this is one of the changes that occurred in my classroom through technology that I am quite proud of.

I can't say as much for my students' poor grammar skills when they contribute to online discussions. As English teachers, we know that texting has contributed to the downfall of our students' grammar and spelling skills; I noticed when I first stepped into the classroom that it would be a constant battle that will continue with each day that technology advances.

When the iPads first arrived, our team of teachers involved with the technology had a lengthy discussion on grammar; all of us feared that the integration of technology would further erode our students' ability to capitalize the pronoun, I, or place apostrophes in their appropriate places. We really did not lay out a strict battle plan on how to combat it; we simply shared that we should try to observe whether or not our students' grammar skills improved or weakened this year.

I am quite lax about my students' grammar in chat rooms. When it comes to the integration of the devices, I try to teach my students appropriate and inappropriate times to use what I once coined "illegal texting language." My students know that, when we are in an informal environment, such as a chat room, they can use text lingo if they wish. They also know that if they use it, I will poke fun at it as well.

For graded assignments or formal assignments, however, I make it clear to my students that I will penalize them for careless grammar mistakes. That is, if they have an error that they easily should have caught with simple proofreading, it will affect their grade. My students have responded to this, and it works well.

There are so many communication and collaboration tools available on both the Web and in the App Store. I have used some to change-up my delivery of content, and students have used others to communicate and collaborate with one another. In addition, there are new ways in which I have communicated with my students.

Neat Chat

Neat Chat is a great website that allows users to create a chat room. When you visit neatchat.com, you are asked to type in a nickname to start a group. From there, the site creates a chat room and a hyperlink at the top of the page. This hyperlink is the code for your chat room; students must type in this hyperlink to get into the room. The hyperlink will look like this:

http://www.neatchat.com/?id=299d8d01302064c7577ef9a5f60544fe

As you can see, the hyperlinks are typically 30 characters long. If each student were to try to type in the hyperlink on their own, it would take about 80 years to get the whole class to the Neat Chat, or any other chat room, for that matter.

The app RedLaser works well with any website's long hyperlinks. I copy and paste the hyperlink into the bar at the website, createqrcode.appspot.com, it converts it to a QR code, and then students scan the QR code I project on the board with the app (Figure 7.1). It makes going to any chat room an easy experience that takes a couple of minutes.

I have created Neat Chat rooms for a few activities. When writing thesis statements, I have had students post their own to the Neat Chat. From there, I can quickly view it and give live feedback to students about the thesis statements they post. Figure 7.2 shows a Neat Chat room after class has ended.

This brings up one of the greatest benefits of chat rooms. Since students post their work live for me to see, I can quickly view it and give them immediate feedback. Before, I would spend a great deal of class time calling up students to my desk or roving around the room to check thesis statements. With Neat Chat, however, I can view it, read it, and tell them if it works or what needs changed.

I have also used Neat Chat for students to ask questions and comments during my lectures. I have also had online discussion periods; I would pose questions, and students and I would engage in conversations in the chat room. All in all, Neat Chat is a great tool to quickly view short samples of student work or engage in online discussions over texts.

FIGURE 7.1 QR code

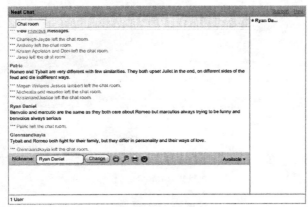

FIGURE 7.2 Neat Chat

Padlet

If you are looking for a communication tool that has a few more features, Padlet is a fantastic tool. Formerly known as Wallwisher, Padlet works similarly to Neat Chat; however, Padlet allows users to upload links to other websites, post pictures, and add video clips onto its website.

Thus, while I have used each tool with my students to spice up communication in the classroom, I prefer to use Padlet. The way in which I have used Padlet with my students is pretty simple; my students will typically use it to provide examples of a specific literary element from a text we read. Or, I will ask students to comment on a specific section of a text we have just read. From there, I will read student answers and use that as a launch pad for live discussion.

To give an example, while reading *The Crucible*, I wanted to quickly review theme with my students. We had discussed it quite a few times throughout the course of the school year; thus, I simply wanted to review the definition and have students post a theme onto a Padlet page. From there, I can quickly give each student feedback, as right when they post, I can tell them whether their theme statement is correct or needs work (Figure 7.3). It's a great way to give students immediate feedback.

To create a wall, I simply go to the website, padlet.com, build a wall, and then title the wall. In the description, I usually give some type of directive; I post what I want students to do on the wall. From there, I create a QR code to the wall. Students scan the board, open the website, double-tap on the wall, type in their name, and respond to a question or instruction.

As I have stated, I like Padlet because students have a few options. They can type in their answers via the keyboard, more outgoing students can post a video, and creative students can post a picture or video response. Figures 7.4–7.6

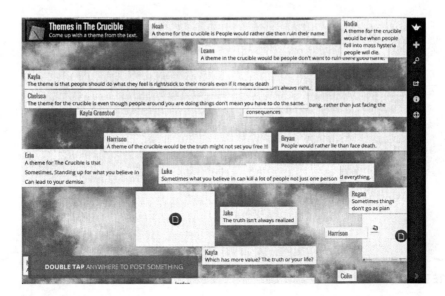

FIGURE 7.3 Padlet

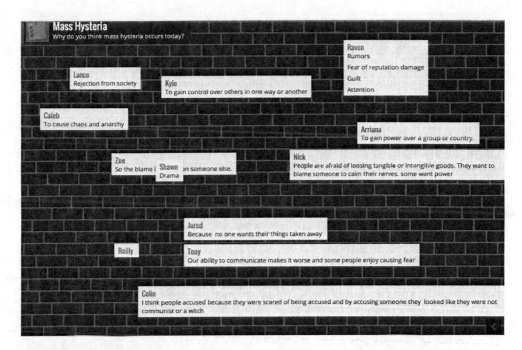

FIGURE 7.4 Padlet typed responses

FIGURE 7.5 Padlet student video response

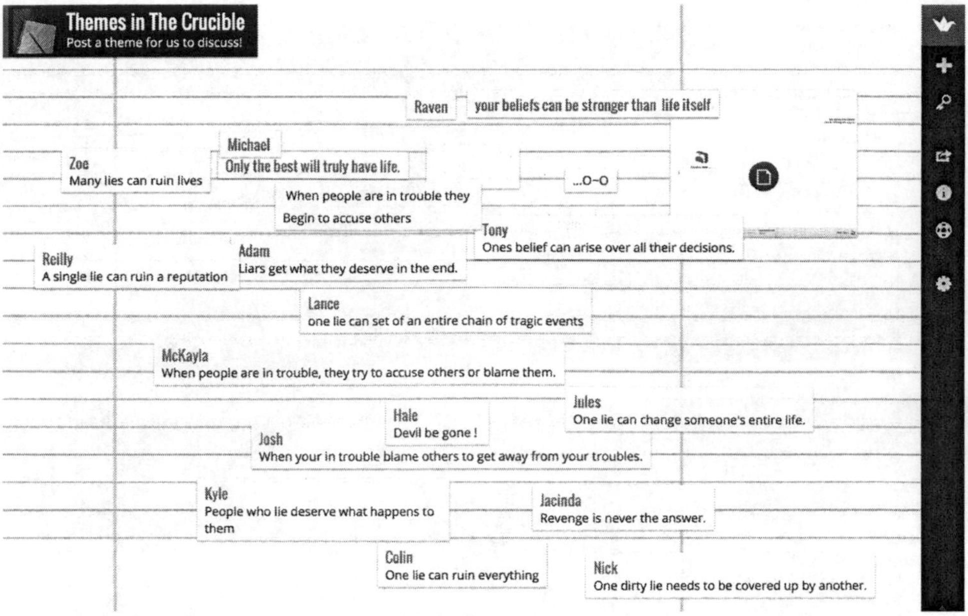

FIGURE 7.6 Padlet

illustrate the different discussions and responses that teachers can hold in a Padlet room. It appeals to many different types of learners, although most students tend to simply type text. These different options make Padlet one of the best communication/discussion tools to use in the classroom.

TodaysMeet

If you want a tool that is both simplistic but also forces students to be concise, todaysmeet.com is a fantastic tool to use in the classroom. TodaysMeet is a chat room in which students are limited to 140-character responses. Once students open up a room, they type in a name and can respond to a discussion question (Figures 7.7 and 7.8). I have used this several times as an opening to a lesson; I will pose a question, and students will then respond. From there, I ask students to elaborate in live discussion.

When it comes to Padlet, TodaysMeet, and Neat Chat, I have found that it works best to have students open these sites *after* I give directions for a particular assignment or discussion; there have been numerous times in which I have talked and students post their comments before I give them directions to do so. This can be quite annoying, as some students are unaware of how rude it is. If this happens to you, simply ask your students to close their iPads until you are done speaking or give them access to the website after you give directions. In addition, it is important to tell students to use their first names in the classroom. Students will want to use nicknames. It's important to use true names, as it will discourage students from typing something that is inappropriate. In addition, because these

FIGURE 7.7 TodaysMeet

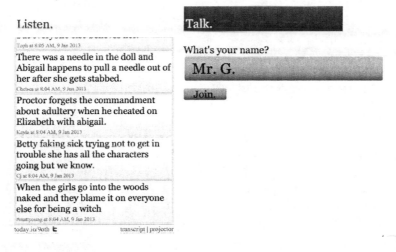

FIGURE 7.8 TodaysMeet

are websites that others can view (albeit difficultly, because they will need the full Web address), I tell students to only use their first name when using these chat rooms. This ensures at least some privacy.

Schoology Course Discussions

One of the things you need to be aware of when it comes to these chat rooms is that they are not exactly easy to find the day after they are used. Thus, if you want to discuss a topic with students and also want to revisit the discussion to

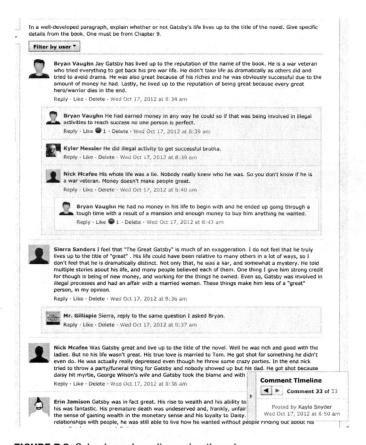

FIGURE 7.9 Schoology class discussion thread

assess in some manner, Schoology discussions work best (Figure 7.9). If you have a Schoology course, you only need to create a discussion. Once you have created a discussion in Schoology, students can post responses by either typing on the iPad's keyboard or they can upload a response via video. I find that Schoology discussions work best when I need to visit the discussion at a later date; all I need to do is log in to Schoology to find the discussion rather than find a neatchat.com or padlet.com URL.

Twitter

A majority of my students already have their own Twitter account; I even know of a few teachers who will tweet class reminders to their students. It can also be used for a quick discussion in the classroom.

I have used it while reading plays with my students, specifically *Romeo and Juliet*. When reading Shakespeare's play, I have asked students to create nightly tweets as a character to demonstrate their understanding of what happened in the text and how their selected character might react to those events. The next day, I would project my Twitter feed either through my desktop computer or via my iPad through Apple TV. From there, I would read particular tweets. After I read the tweet, we would discuss it.

To implement Twitter, I spent about 20 minutes of class time having my students set up accounts through their school e-mail. To view their tweets, I then had to follow my students' accounts via my Twitter account. To ensure privacy and that our school Twitter accounts would remain private, we also made our Twitter accounts private. Outsiders could still try to follow students, but I told them not to accept these requests. I was able to monitor this, as I could easily see who they were following.

It is important to note that when students activate a new Twitter account, they *must* confirm their account via e-mail. My students have run into the problem of their accounts becoming suspended due to the fact that they did not verify their new accounts in their e-mail. Thus, make sure your students do this.

When it comes to using social networking in the classroom, I try to be as cautious as possible. Since Twitter is somewhat private, as long as students are not following strangers, I do put my guard up and check student accounts on a weekly basis to see who they are following. This is to ensure that students understand that social networking in the classroom is used to learn; if students want to use Twitter for entertainment, they can set up an account at home with their personal e-mail accounts.

From an assessment standpoint, viewing all the tweets allowed me to assess both characterization and plot; by reading their responses, I could clearly see which students understood what we read, which understood their character and what happened to them that day, and which students needed certain events clarified.

Collaborating with Schoology Groups

One of the perks of the Schoology social networking website is that teachers can create group pages for students to collaborate, upload documents and videos, and share ideas for any length of time.

I typically create group pages for any lengthy group assignment; I will put students in groups (usually labeled one through however many groups there are). For each group, I create Schoology groups for students to use as a starting point to communicate and collaborate.

All they need to access the group page is the eight-digit access code in the bottom left of the group page. With this access code, only students in that group can create and upload content; nobody else can access the group without the group's code. The only person who has access to this code is the creator of the group, and I create all groups.

I like Schoology groups because they allow students to privately work together without outsiders interfering. As the creator of each group, I am given updates on each group whenever I log in. I like that I am able to monitor the content on each page as well.

One of the added benefits of Schoology groups is that they allow students to contribute to group work when they are not available in class. During a

——————————————————————————————————— Most Recent ▼

Autumn Bianchi
Sorry I'm not at school but one idea is that maybe Aaron and Alex are fighting criticizing each other showing the Sherman vs. Ewing thing... Just an initial idea so we can tweak it if we need to
Fri Jan 25, 2013 at 6:02 am Comment · Like

Brandon Springer
The Black Death, illness.
Wed Jan 23, 2013 at 1:32 pm Comment · Like

Brandon Springer
Hg wells public announcement of the war of worlds. Was actually broadcasted and cause actual panic!!!!!!!!!!!!!

FIGURE 7.10 Schoology group discussions

three-week project-based learning assignment, one group's member was not in class. She still wanted to contribute to the group, so she ended up posting a comment on her group's page (Figure 7.10). As a result, she was able to contribute and have her voice heard even though she was not in class.

Sub Videos and Lessons Posted to Schoology Courses

Technology has even allowed me to change the way in which I collaborate with my students when I can't be in class. Whenever I anticipate an absence, whether it is professional development or a personal day, I will use the camera on my iPad and film a video for my students explaining what they are to do that day. I typically film a greeting, the assignment, and remind them that they can post any questions about the assignment in the comments area under the video. From there, I upload the video and any other necessary attachments to our class's Schoology page. With this video, the only items I leave with the sub are my seating charts for him or her to take attendance each period.

When students come into class on a day I am absent, the sub tells them to open up their Schoology pages and complete the assignment that is uploaded. Students complete it and e-mail or upload these assignments to me. If anything hinders the completion of the assignment, they are to comment underneath my sub video on our Schoology page.

The greatest perk of this change in routine is that I know that my directives will be given to my students via video. I have not had any issues with students not understanding directions; if they need clarification, they can ask in the comments section, and I can either respond to them if my iPad is available or clarify the next day. Overall, it's a great way for me to be in the classroom when I physically can't be present.

Schoology Informational Text Discussion Threads

One of my favorite ways of communicating with students is through the use of weekly discussions. A way in which I hold weekly discussions is through the use of discussion posts over informational articles on Schoology. I don't know about you, but I feel that, throughout the course of the school year, I have trouble implementing informational texts in my lessons on a regular basis. Yes, I will teach units that focus primarily on important informational and persuasive texts from history, but these units are typically short.

To implement more reading of informational texts in my classroom, I decided to create an assignment I call "Schoology Informational Text Discussion Threads." I find an informational text online, post a link to it as a discussion on a class's Schoology course, and students then have a week to create a formal discussion post. In their discussion post, they are to summarize the article and react to the article. I create a rubric to assess their ability to analyze the article, integrate textual evidence, use correct spelling/grammar, and contribute to the discussion thread throughout the week. It has helped me to remain consistent with teaching informational texts, as teaching nonfiction is important as well.

Video Diaries with the Camera Roll

While reading *The Adventures of Huckleberry Finn* with my college prep students, one of the essential questions I asked was whether or not the novel has racist undertones. We discussed at length in the beginning of the unit why the book is banned. I also found a fantastic *60 Minutes* segment about the publication of the novel in which the "n word" is replaced with the word "slave."

I then had students read Chapter 1 and begin a video diary, similar to one you might see in a reality show. Students, upon reading certain sections,

FIGURE 7.11 Video diary

explained whether or not they thought Twain was racist. They also had to give specific evidence to explain their reasoning. Upon completion of the novel, students posted their own live video diaries throughout the unit on Schoology (Figure 7.11). Then, at the end of the novel, they reviewed their diaries to see if their opinion had changed.

AnswerGarden

Another tool that I have used to change the way in which students communicate with me is through the website answergarden.ch. The website is a bit different from other chat rooms my students have used in the past.

The website is pretty simplistic; I go to answergarden.ch, create an AnswerGarden, and from there, type in a topic or question. I then give students access to the room like any other chat room, through the use of a QR code. From there, students answer the question. As I refresh the page, new answers appear. The more students that type in the same response, the larger the text appears on my screen.

Thus, I use this as a way for students to directly tell me concepts they understand and concepts they feel may need to review. Right before the state tests, I tend to review concepts with them. I will open up an AnswerGarden to see exactly which concepts each particular class feels they need to review (Figure 7.12). Once again, it's not the most formal way of obtaining student data, but it's a nice way to see how the class as a whole feels about their knowledge and weaknesses. If you use AnswerGarden, make sure that you either give students a question with numerous one- or two-word responses, as I have found it works best with these types of questions.

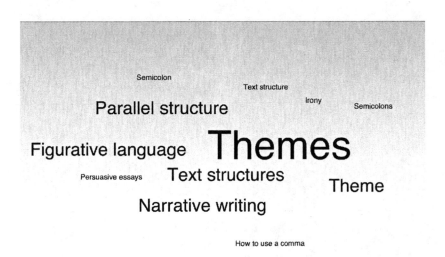

FIGURE 7.12 AnswerGarden

Conclusion

Whether it is Neat Chat, Padlet, or the Camera Roll, the iPad opens up numerous amounts of communication and collaboration tools to its users. My students primarily use these tools to ask questions during lectures. In addition, I have used them to put students in groups and to give my introverted students an outlet to contribute to class discussions.

We do not replace actual talking and live discussion with typing in chat rooms. I use these tools to begin the discussion; I will point out interesting comments in the classroom, ask students to elaborate on their ideas, and press other students to clarify vague comments. Between this dialogue and the dialogue that occurs with these tools and apps, all students are communicating more than ever before, as they have new and exciting ways to do so.

Whether they are communicating in a formal or informal manner, these communication and collaboration bring a new dynamic to the classroom. With these tools and the fact that class discussion is online, my students are writing more than in past years. Their writing may not be grammatically correct 100% of the time, but I have noticed that students of all levels and backgrounds contribute to class discussions. This is because students no longer have to raise their hand and speak. They can speak through typing on the iPad. This has also resulted in more voices speaking up in my class that would have otherwise been silent.

8

Transforming Public Speaking

While there are many resources available to update the ELA classroom, I initially had trouble figuring out how to update my Speech class. Outside of the Camera Roll and taping students' speeches, I initially could not find many apps to change the way I taught the class and make it interactive.

Whereas many of the reading and writing apps appear as if they are geared toward the ELA classroom, I knew I would have to be creative when incorporating the technology to my Speech students. I would have to find tools and figure out how those could be woven into instruction to enhance the class and better prepare my students for their speeches. This took more time than I would have hoped.

That is part of the reason why I consider the first semester of using the iPads with my Speech students a disappointment. I take full blame for it as well. When we wrote our grant, we emphasized the importance of the iPads to transform our reading and writing instruction. To be honest, while I used the iPads in some lessons for my Speech class, I was more focused on my English classes. Between this focus and the lack of tools, it took a great deal of time to update this class. Only now, after two years of using iPads in the classroom, I can definitely say that, while it took some time, my students in this class use technology just as much as students in my English classes.

This is a point that I want to stress. When I speak to other educators, and they realize the abundance of tools available to transform their teaching, they can quickly become overwhelmed and not know where to begin. My advice when it comes to this is to take it one tool/app/lesson at a time. This is what I did with my Speech class, and finally, after two years, I have a created a class in which the technology aids instruction on a regular basis. Regardless of whether you teach a public speaking course or not, some of these tools can be of use to you, as the Common Core Standards definitely put more emphasis on students acquiring speaking and listening skills. Therefore, I am rolling out some of these ideas and apps in my English classes when students need to give oral presentations.

Preparing for Speeches with the Camera Roll

One of the first tools I used, and one of the most beneficial tools that is available on the iPad for my Speech students, is the Camera Roll. Before the iPads arrived, I would always tell my students that one of the best things they can do to prepare for a speech is to record themselves and watch the recording. I say this because with the Camera Roll, students can see their strengths and weaknesses as orators for themselves. Before, students relied on both their peers and me to critique their speeches. With the Camera Roll, they are now able to critique themselves as they practice their speeches.

As a result, I always reserve the day before students give their speeches for them to pair up with somebody, record one another's speeches, upload them to Schoology, and then watch them. Figure 8.1 illustrates one student as she prepares for her upcoming speech. From there, students submit a paragraph or create a video diary in which they explain what they need to work on before they give their speech. While many students do not like watching themselves on the iPad (it definitely takes a while for them to get used to it), they have found that this is a way for them to see firsthand what they need to work on.

Uploading and Watching Speeches

I also record students while they give their actual speeches live in front of the class. When students give their speeches, they give their assigned iPad to a friend to record. From there, students give their speeches, and once they finish delivering it, they then take their recording and upload it to a Schoology assignment I create before class. From there, underneath their postings, students will submit a five-paragraph critique of their own speech. In addition, their

FIGURE 8.1 Speech practice

classmates also have an opportunity to type in constructive criticism. This, in turn, creates a discussion board in which students have meaningful conversations about one another's speeches. Overall, by uploading videos, students are able to see their own strengths and weaknesses and critique themselves and others' speeches as well.

We have encountered some problems with uploading. Some students' speeches are so long that the file size of their video is too large to post on Schoology. I have students upload one or two sections of their speeches and critique what they are able to upload. While this is a nuisance, each student is still able to upload and critique at least two to three minutes of their speeches.

Video Critiques

I also have tried to have students create video critiques during class. After students delivered their actual introduction speeches, I asked them to write a five-paragraph critique for homework. The next day, students used their iPad and read their critique to their iPad to further practice effective pitch, rate, volume, eye contact, and gestures (Figure 8.2). It was a way for students to practice public speaking and yet another chance for students to work on their weaknesses.

However, with only a class set of iPads, my students encountered one main problem with this assignment. When students sat at their desks and tried taping themselves reading their critiques, the classroom became too loud for anyone to focus, let alone hear their critique on the iPad. Therefore, I asked half of the students to go out into the hallway to record and the other half to stay inside the classroom. This alleviated some of the problem, but students who did not speak loudly still could not be heard on the iPad.

FIGURE 8.2 Video critique

This addresses a big problem when it comes to only having a class set of iPads. When I ask students to record into the iPad in one classroom, the environment is too loud for anyone to concentrate. In turn, the audio is quite poor; I also feel terrible asking some students to go in the hallway, as the potential to distract other teachers' classes increases. This is frustrating, as this assignment holds a lot of value; it gives students yet another chance to practice vocal quality and nonverbal clues. However, it simply is not feasible in one classroom. Therefore, this assignment works best for a 1:1 environment in which students have their own iPads and complete it for homework.

Practicing Vocal Quality with QuickVoice

To help students with their pitch, rate, and volume, I have asked them to record themselves using the QuickVoice app. With this app, students can record their voices, and from there, can listen to their recordings and send them to me via e-mail (Figure 8.3).

I initially used this app as a pre-assessment with my Speech students. When the semester begins, I have them read famous speeches (americanrhetoric.com is a fantastic website to obtain speeches; it is a speech library), and from there, they listen and evaluate their pitch, rate, and volume. From there, they practice until they have a recording that they like, which they then e-mail to me to listen to.

I also use this app throughout the course of the semester. With a storytelling unit, students can practice reading fairy tales and other children's stories with the app. We first discuss the qualities of a great narrator, examine narrations from YouTube, and analyze character voices and how to convey emotions. Once students select a story from a Google search, they practice their reading, and use

FIGURE 8.3 QuickVoice

QuickVoice to record. Once they have recorded, they then evaluate the pitch, rate, and volume of their narration, as well as character voices.

Finally, I use the app one final time during a debate unit. My students use the app when they prepare for their debates; they record how they might present information to practice speaking with conviction.

Once again, a drawback to the app is that, when you have so many students trying to record into an app at once, it can make for a loud classroom environment. Therefore, for any assignment with the app, I usually ask students to work with a partner. Each pair will use two iPads; one iPad will contain the story, and the other will have the QuickVoice app open. While the student who is recording will read their story from the iPad, the partner will hold the other iPad for the student to speak clearly to the iPad's microphone. I also ask half the pairs to go out in the hallway, and half stay in the classroom. This eliminates the amount of people speaking at a given time; as a result, the iPad's microphone can record the speaker's voice and not the background noise. Obviously, these assignments will work much better when they can take their iPad home.

Another drawback to the app entails e-mailing. The free version of the app does not allow users to e-mail files more than 5MB in size. Therefore, when using the app, students must limit their recordings to about two minutes. Therefore, I usually ask students to keep their recordings at about three minutes. That way, I can ensure that I receive an e-mail to grade.

In terms of grouping with the app, I usually find that it works best to pair a shy student with someone who is more outgoing. When it comes to giving speeches, many shy students have trouble with their vocal quality. Therefore, the more outgoing student can coach the shy student. Since the shy student has a base knowledge of effective pitch, rate, and volume, he/she can mentor the outgoing student as well.

Some students definitely struggle watching themselves on video through the Camera Roll and hearing their voices with the QuickVoice app. I do not blame them; I always hated watching myself or hearing my own voice. It took a great deal of time to become used to it myself. However, the learning experience is undeniable. I cannot count how many times I have heard students say, "I did not know that I did that" while watching or listening to themselves. From there, we have valuable discussions on how students can work through individual nervous ticks, vocal hindrances, and issues with lack of gestures or body language. The fact that students are seeing themselves speak has definitely changed the dynamic of the class.

Demonstration Speeches, Infomercials, iMovie, and Keynote

One of my students' favorite assignments in Speech class entails creating an infomercial. As part of a demonstration Speech unit, students learn how to vary their vocal quality and nonverbals when trying to sell something to an audience. They also learn how to give clear and precise step-by-step instructions on how to use a product.

Way back when I first taught the class, I assigned this as a live presentation. Students had to present their infomercials live to the class. I graded them on their vocal quality, nonverbal cues, and clarity of the actual demonstration.

As the presence of technology increased in my school, I would check out Flip Video cameras from my school's library for students to record actual infomercials. While I liked the Flip Video cameras, as they were easy to use, they did not allow for complex editing. As a result, many of the products students created with these cameras did not exactly look like infomercials. The only truly great infomercials were created by groups that had access to their own video-editing software at home or through our school's broadcasting program.

The amount of times I have used iMovie with all of my students definitely makes it worth the purchase. With iMovie, students are able to add text to videos, import pictures from the Camera Roll, add music and sound effects, and so much more. As a result, students went above and beyond as they edited their film pieces together. In fact, students also used another app, Keynote, to create images and backgrounds true to the style of an infomercial. Figures 8.4–8.6 truly show the creativity students exude with this project.

We usually spend a week working on this project. Students spent the first day scripting/outlining in their groups. They spend the next day storyboarding. They spend another day recording. They spend the last two days editing clips and creating effects. We then spend a final day watching each group's infomercial on the projector.

Overall, students tend to be excited, engaged, and ultimately enjoy this assignment. They saw the value of public speaking; with this assignment, they realized that what they learn in the class when it comes to vocal quality, audience, nonverbal cues, etc. spreads to anything they see on television, as they must use these features to engage an audience. Throughout the course of the semester, students will ask me if they can watch their infomercials again. This lets me know that the assignment is successful when it comes to student motivation.

FIGURE 8.4 Speech infomercial project

FIGURE 8.5 Speech infomercial project

FIGURE 8.6 Speech infomercial project

Critiquing Speeches

With the arrival of the technology, one of the changes my school's administration made was to open up YouTube to the school. Prior to the usage of iPads, our school blocked YouTube, as some of the videos and user comments are inappropriate. I initially thought that this would create problems in the classroom. I thought it would create yet another distraction. However, it really has not created a distraction, especially when I have lessons/activities in which students are working bell to bell. If students are not busy, they will find a way to entertain themselves with the iPad. One of the first places they go to is YouTube. Therefore, if you do not want your students to surf YouTube, make sure there is not downtime.

One of the most beneficial aspects of YouTube is that I can find examples of speeches, and we can then critique them. I try to find examples of speeches from either YouTube or past student samples, post them to our class's Schoology page, and as we watch the video, students will type their critique of the speaker underneath the video (Figure 8.7).

Another way in which students have critiqued speeches is by critiquing one another in chat rooms. I reserve each Monday in Speech class for impromptu speeches. Each student, throughout the course of the semester, is to give two one-minute impromptu speeches and one two-minute impromptu speech. Each Monday, about four or five students give their speech. I usually take volunteers first, and then I will call on random people from my grade book.

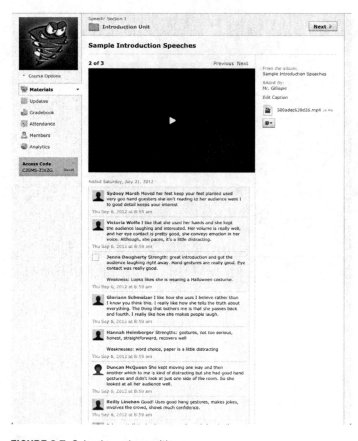

FIGURE 8.7 Schoology class critique

I assign the student a topic, and he or she has one chance to veto. If they veto the first topic, they are stuck with the next topic they are given. They then have about two to three minutes to prepare a speech that is organized, and has an introduction, a thesis, a body, and a conclusion. It must have appropriate vocal quality, gestures, and eye contact.

Once the speaker gives his or her speech, I immediately assign the next student a speech. While that next person is preparing his or her speech, we critique the previous speaker using the website neatchat.com (Figure 8.8). To do so, students type in one strength or weakness in the chat room. We then discuss, and if some comments are unclear or vague, I ask for clarification during live discussion.

To switch things up a bit, once the second semester begins, I substitute neatchat.com for todaysmeet.com. TodaysMeet is a similar website, and I use it in the same way as Neat Chat. Before class, I create a TodaysMeet room, create a QR code, and students can then critique speakers. The only difference is that TodaysMeet works in the same vein as Twitter; students can type in responses no longer than 140 characters at a time. This works a bit better, as students must make clear and concise critiques (Figure 8.9).

When it comes to both Neat Chat and TodaysMeet, I ask students to do three things. First, they use their first name and last initial when typing in their name. This way, I can see who typed in what responses. Second, I can't stress the importance of asking students to close their iPads when a speaker is delivering his or her impromptu speech. Some students will try surfing the Web when students are speaking. Finally, I ask that students solely type in critiques and do not have side conversations.

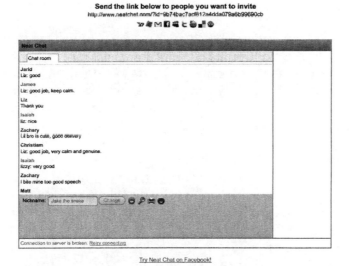

FIGURE 8.8 Neat Chat critique

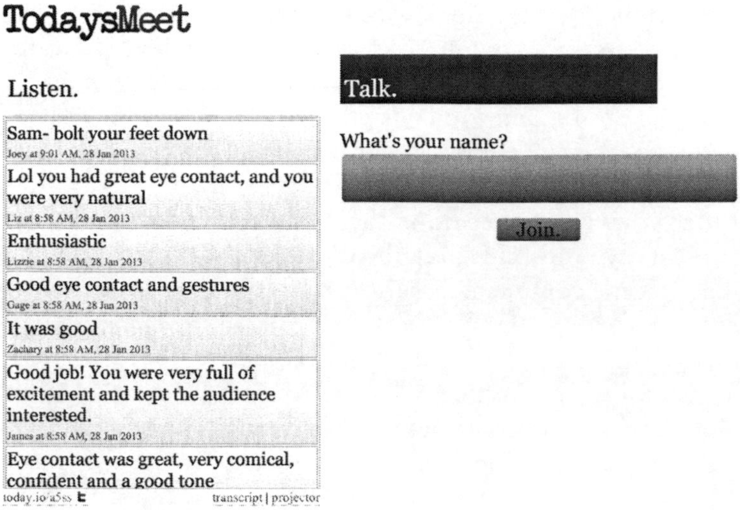

TodaysMeet

Listen.

Sam- bolt your feet down
Joey at 9:01 AM, 28 Jan 2013
Lol you had great eye contact, and you were very natural
Liz at 8:58 AM, 28 Jan 2013
Enthusiastic
Lizzie at 8:58 AM, 28 Jan 2013
Good eye contact and gestures
Gage at 8:58 AM, 28 Jan 2013
It was good
Zachary at 8:58 AM, 28 Jan 2013
Good job! You were very full of excitement and kept the audience interested.
James at 8:58 AM, 28 Jan 2013
Eye contact was great, very comical, confident and a good tone

today.io/a5ss ⬚   transcript | projector

Talk.

What's your name?

Join.

FIGURE 8.9 TodaysMeet critique

Transforming the Storytelling Speech Unit

Another unit I always look forward to teaching and that students enjoy is storytelling. Students tend to enjoy this unit, as it is a departure from informative and persuasive speaking. While there are websites and resources to help English teachers use apps in the classroom, there are not many to help speech teachers implement this technology with specific units. With a lot of research, there are many apps available to allow students to practice their delivery of different stories.

The final assessment for this unit is for students to deliver an interpretation of a fairy tale live in front of their classmates. We first analyze what makes for a suitable selection, how to narrate, and how to distinguish different characters through the use of vocal quality, facial expressions, body language, and gestures. Thus, all of the activities outlined below are designed to help students deliver a fairy tale effectively live in front of their classmates.

There are many apps available to formatively assess students on each of these qualities. I usually like to begin the unit by discussing how to narrate. We take a look at some narrations on YouTube (typing in "storytelling speeches" into YouTube will generate some examples), and from there, we generate a list of qualities of an effective narrator via TodaysMeet. From there, students then open up the app called A Story Before Bed. This app is one of my favorite apps I have ever used with my students.

The way the app works is simple. First, the user must create an account and verify it via e-mail. Once students have done this, the app then takes them to the home screen. From there, you have two choices: you can either record a book, or you can view your past recordings, if you have any. Once you select a book to record, you can type in your name and who you are reading the book to. From there, you can hit the record button and record the story. Figure 8.10 shows a finished product of a story two students read aloud. Once you are finished, you can e-mail it to any person you would like. That person then receives a hyperlink to the story's recording that can only be viewed from an actual computer. It's important to note that these recordings cannot be opened and viewed from an iPad, but rather, a desktop computer or laptop. Once the website opens, you can view the recorder reading the story to the camera. The pages to the story flip as the recorder reads the selection.

It is an amazing app, and like the apps that have been most successful in my classroom, it is geared directly toward this storytelling unit. Students had a blast with the app as well. We spent a day watching everyone's recordings. They e-mailed their recordings to me, and I then posted the links under a Schoology assignment for everyone to view. We then discussed the strengths and weaknesses of each speaker, and this gave each speaker feedback as they prepared for their final storytelling speech.

As the storytelling unit progressed and we discussed developing characters, we used two puppet apps, Puppet Pals and Sock Puppets, to practice character voices. While students in my English classes have used them for certain lessons, I find that these two apps are definitely more appropriate for a storytelling unit. Once students have selected a fairy tale they will present to the class for their final storytelling speech, I give them time to practice both narrating and character voices with the Puppet Pals app (Figure 8.11). They then annotate their story with notes on vocal quality.

From there, they select characters that best match the characters in their story, record their narration, and upload it to our Schoology page for others to critique

FIGURE 8.10 A Story Before Bed

FIGURE 8.11 Puppet Pals

and give feedback. This helps students as they prepare to deliver this speech live in front of their classmates, as they can watch firsthand what their vocal quality is like and make adjustments.

Notes, Keynote, and Apple TV

The iPad is changing education, and I fully believe that it is changing the landscape of public speaking. When I first taught the class, students delivered extemporaneous speeches in which they were allowed a note card with a word limit. This encouraged students to know the content of their speech and to deliver it in a conversational manner.

While I still encourage extemporaneous speaking, I do encourage students to use technology as they speak. They are allowed a visual aid that enhances a certain part of their speech; I discourage visual aids that play throughout the duration of their speech. It can be distracting, and I want each student's audience to focus on them, not a visual aid.

With Apple TV, Notes, and Keynote, I encourage students to use their iPad when they deliver speeches (Figure 8.12). When students deliver their informative and persuasive speeches, I encourage them to write their notes they use for their speech using the iPad's Notes app. This acts as the note card they would typically bring up with them as they deliver their speeches. From there, students can create a visual aid with the Keynote app; this is the equivalent to PowerPoint on the iPad. From there, students can project their visual aid using Apple TV.

I do not require students to use their iPads when they speak, as it is quite bulky and can be distracting for them and their audience. I recommend that students use the method that makes them most comfortable in the front of the room.

FIGURE 8.12 Speaking with an iPad

Many students still prefer a note card, as it is easier for students to handle. Overall, the best thing for public speakers is to be comfortable and relaxed when they are delivering their speeches; thus, I give them the option that best suits them.

Persuasion, Debating, and Skype

Outside of the Internet and basic research, one useful app that students have used to prepare for debates and persuasive speeches is the Pro/Con T-Chart app. With this app, students can begin identifying the pros and cons for any argument. It is a nice way for students to begin outlining their arguments; from there, students know exactly what their arguments will be and have a beginning point to refute their opponents' arguments.

As much of a cliché as it may sound, with the iPad, there really are no limits when it comes to public speaking. With Skype and FaceTime, there is a great chance for students' messages to spread well beyond the four walls of my classroom.

I first implemented Skype in my Speech class during a debate unit. During this unit, we discuss the art of rhetoric, fallacies of thinking, and the structure of a debate. Once I feel that they understand how to create logical arguments and refute others, we then hold a practice debate. Students get into groups of four, I divide them into teams of two, give them a proposition, and they then research and prepare for their debate. Then, in one class period, the groups debate one another, and I walk around, noticing strengths and weaknesses.

The day before the practice debates, a student informed me that she had a funeral to attend. Not wanting to let her partner down, she volunteered to Skype in during the class, as she would be available during the class period.

FIGURE 8.13 Debating with Skype

FIGURE 8.14 Debating with Skype

FIGURE 8.15 Debating with Skype

I then had them set up Skype accounts and test call one another. On the day of the practice debates, she called her partner and was able to deliver her parts of the debate. Her partner was also able to take the iPad with her across the hall during a work period and discuss what to say in the next sections of the debate (Figures 8.13–8.15). It was a really neat experience.

We took this to another level during the class's summative debates. I decided it was time to vary the audience for my students. As the semester neared its end, at the end of a debate unit, I decided to have students debate in front of a study hall in our school's theater. Many students definitely illustrated their trepidation when I first announced this assignment. However, one of the problems I have noticed while teaching this class is that students become too comfortable and familiar with one another; as a result, they lose their speech anxiety. While I take pride in the fact that many students gain confidence, my main goal with this class is that students can cope and succeed in any speaking environment.

Conclusion

While it may have taken a while, I feel as if my Speech class has caught up with my English classes when it comes to using the iPads on a daily basis. From the Camera Roll to Puppet Pals, there are different apps and resources for students to practice for summative speeches, critique their own speeches, and critique others.

That being addressed, there is still another way to transform the class. With the iPad's FaceTime and Skype apps, the potential to broaden the audience in Speech class definitely makes the future of public speaking truly exciting. One of my next goals with this ability is to pair up with another Speech teacher and have our students give speeches to one another. Or, the potential is there to have my students deliver a speech with another person via Skype. With this ability, students can spread a positive message well beyond the four walls of the classroom.

CHAPTER

9

Differentiating Instruction with iPads

I don't know about you, but differentiation is one of the areas of my teaching that, no matter how cognizant I am of it when planning my lessons, I always feel like it is my weakest area as a teacher. As much as I try to tailor lessons to what students already know, their learning styles, interests, and more, I feel that, if a student scores lowly on a test or quiz, I did not differentiate enough to ensure that individual learned the content he or she needed to learn.

I attribute this attitude toward differentiation to the fact that it is so widely stressed at the university level. When studying to become a teacher, I was constantly told that I must differentiate to meet the needs of *all* learners. In my experience, this was engrained in me, but I was never taught many pedagogically sound strategies to differentiate. It is no wonder I always feel as if I fail when it comes to differentiation in my classroom, let alone how to do it with technology such as an iPad.

Thus, I decided to research this a bit more while studying for my master's in Curriculum and Instruction. I completed an action research project. During this process, I primarily sifted through the research of Carol Ann Tomlinson. According to Tomlinson, differentiation occurs when a teacher "systematically modifies content, process or product based on students' readiness for the particular topic, materials, or skills; personal interests; and learning profiles" (Tomlinson, 1999: 14). In my classroom, I differentiate my instructional and assessment methods based on students' prior knowledge, interests, and learning styles. The iPad has created a new dynamic to this differentiation in my classroom; many Web tools and apps can help students in different areas in which they struggle or excel.

Pre-assessments with Socrative

With all the different testing apps and tools on the iPad, gathering data for each student is easier now than it has ever been. Thus, as teachers, we can use tools such as Socrative and Schoology tests to gather information about students. We can do so right on the first days of school with our students to understand what they know right from the get-go.

Thus, one of the first tasks I complete with my students before each unit is a pre-assessment with Socrative on the iPad. Instead of giving students a worksheet to see what they know, I will ask students to complete a pre-assessment covering specific literary terms and concepts via Socrative.

Pre-assessments that I create via Socrative are mostly multiple-choice questions with a few short-answer questions. When I begin a Socrative pre-assessment, I tell students that if they do not know the answer for short-answer questions, to simply write, "I don't know" in the text box. From there, students finish the pre-assessment, I end the session, and the app will send me a report with students' answers. For the multiple-choice questions, if students answer the question correctly, it is highlighted in the spreadsheet in green. If they miss the question, it is highlighted in red. This color-coded spreadsheet makes figuring out which students know what easier than before.

In addition, I usually give formative assessments throughout a unit to gage student knowledge. Socrative is a fantastic choice to give these types of assessments. For someone such as me, who is a visual learner, the color-coding allows me to clearly see what students know and do not know. All in all, Socrative pre-assessments and data give me a visual representation to see exactly what students know before I begin a unit. It also allows me to identify students who know quite a bit going into a unit and those who are not familiar with concepts. This can help me as I create lessons and grouping strategies for activities.

Independent Reading Projects

One of the ways in which I have appealed to students' interests and individual reading levels is through the use of independent reading projects. Usually, during quarters in which we read plays, I have students pick a book of their choice from the library and read it throughout the course of a grading period. I usually give this assignment when we read plays because in my class, we primarily read these types of texts aloud as a class. Thus, the independent reading assignment forces students to read outside of class as well.

To assess students' comprehension of the book, I usually assign two types of tasks. First, students respond to a variety of discussion questions while reading their books. I call these checkpoints. Every two weeks, students must respond to questions that ask them to summarize what they have read, find examples of different literary terms, explain themes, analyze characters, or find other concepts that we find in all literary works. Students respond to these questions in an online forum or Schoology discussion thread before a certain date.

Then, at the end of the quarter, after completing these discussions, students complete a final assignment; using the app of their choice, students have two days to create a product that shows their knowledge of the book. The only stipulation is that they follow the rubric that outlines the standards I want students to master during that specific grading period. I may even place concepts from previous quarters into the rubric as a way of reinforcing previous literary concepts.

I like to give this assignment for a few reasons. First, it allows students to read a book that appeals to them; philosophically, I believe that my job is to foster a love for reading. Quite frankly, many of the required texts that I teach can be, well, quite dry. This is a way to give students a choice in what they read that appeals to their interests. I also find that the ability for students to show their knowledge of the book with the app of their choice allows students to be creative. I find that students have fun with these final projects because they have a choice in how they show their understanding of what they have read, which is a tenet of differentiation.

Once each student has his or her own iPad to take home, I will have students find free iBooks in Apple's iBookstore to read at home on their iPads. Thus, students will not need to visit the library to find a book, unless, of course, this is their preferred method of reading. Moreover, this will give students an opportunity to view more book selections that appeal to their individual interests. All in all, this will bring yet another new dynamic to this type of assignment in my classroom.

Huck Finn Differentiated Product

Aside from their final independent reading project, I have also given students the opportunity to show their knowledge of required readings with the app of their choice. For a summative assessment over *Huck Finn*, my students were in the beginning of the fourth and final quarter of the school year, and our time together with the technology was coming to an end. I wanted to assess students' creativity with the technology and how much they had grown in using it. Therefore, I came up with an assignment in which students could select an app of their choice and teach me about the concepts we learned throughout that unit. I gave them a rubric to follow; my only directive was to show understanding of concepts on the rubric with any app(s) they wanted (Box 9.1).

The fact that they were able to pick any app was, similar to the independent reading project, an assessment in creativity. It also gave students the option to show their knowledge of Twain's novel in the manner that best suited them. Some students created a talk show; some created a mind map. Others created a radio podcast with Audioboo. All in all, it was a great assessment in that it forced students to show their understanding of the novel in a way that also forced them to explore and use many of the apps we had used throughout the year.

Appealing to Multiple Intelligences

Students have their own unique interests and ways of learning. According to Howard Gardner, students "learn, remember, perform, and understand in different ways" (Gardner, 2011: 12). Thus, our job as teachers is to create lessons, activities, and assignments throughout the course of a school year that appeal to the ways in which students best learn. As an English teacher, this can be quite

Box 9.1 *Huck Finn* Summative

Learning Target: I can show my understanding of important literary concepts in a creative/innovative manner.

We have just finished reading the novel, *The Adventures of Huckleberry Finn*. Your final assignment is to show your knowledge of the novel and important literary concepts through the use of an app of your choice. You may work with a partner, take today and tomorrow to plan out, and Wednesday to record/film/finalize your product. The following are apps you can use:

Camera	Audioboo	ShowMe
iMovie	WordCloud	Toontastic
iTellaStory	CloudOn	Popplet
Puppet Pals, etc.	Evernote	Schoology
Songify	Any others you can think of	

Your goal is to show your understanding of the novel with the app using important concepts highlighted in the rubric below. Be creative!

Criteria	5 (Superior)	4 (Proficient)	3 (Average)	2 (Below Proficient)	0 (No/Little Attempt)
Summary of the Novel					
Symbols Explained					
Themes Explained					
Analysis of How Huck Changes					
Analysis of Satire					
Analysis of Why it is Considered a Work of Realism					
Analysis/Understanding of Characters					
Creativity/Innovation of Product					

__/40 Total

difficult at times, especially due to the fact that our main job is to teach students how to read and write. It takes some creativity to teach these skills to students with different learning modalities.

When it comes to all methods of differentiation, the iPad has definitely allowed me to appeal to more types of learners than ever before. There are so many different apps available in the App Store that appeal to my students' individual intelligence levels.

When it comes to reading comprehension, many of my activities involve monitoring student comprehension of a text and students analyzing characterization in a text. Table 9.1 has a list of different learning modalities, apps that support each style of learning, and a brief idea of an assignment with regard to reading comprehension and analyzing characterization in a text. While there are plenty of other reading standards I teach, these are two that are most widely taught in any literature unit. As Table 9.1 shows, there are many different ways to appeal to learning styles with regard to showing comprehension of a text and analyzing literature.

To better understand my students' learning styles, I prefer to type learning style inventories into Socrative quizzes so that I can visually analyze my students' learning styles in reports that the app e-mails as a spreadsheet. This makes it easy for me to analyze the data and see how students learn best. From there, these learning styles can be the basis for grouping; at times, I will group students based on similar learning styles and have them complete a task with an app that is geared toward that specific learning style. Or, if I want students to complete the task on their own, I will have them find an app that appeals to their specific learning modalities.

When it comes to appealing to different learning styles, I will give students a reading assignment for homework. Then, the next day, I will simply give them a choice board that demonstrates the different learning styles and say, "show me what you read last night" or ask them to summarize what they read with the reading choice board (Table 9.2). From there, students pick an element from the choice board, complete the task, and e-mail their products to me or upload them to our Schoology course.

Helping Students with Reading Comprehension

When it comes to the actual task of reading, it is also important to appeal to different types of learners. To do so, I give students options over how they may read books. Visual students read best when they are actually reading the words on a page; this is exactly how I read. However, some students are more auditory learners and need to actually hear to comprehend what they read.

Thus, I allow students to bring in their headphones to class if they want to have the iPad read to them. There are a few ways in which students can listen to books and short stories on the iPad. First, if the text is in our online textbook, students simply need to press the speaker function, as our online textbook already has the option for selections to be read aloud to them.

TABLE 9.1 Learning modalities chart

Learning Style	App	Assignment Idea
Visual/Spatial	Pic Collage	Create a collage over a character, chapter, or entire novel
Musical/Rhythmic	iTellaStory	Write a poem about a character, chapter; write a poem summarizing a reading selection
Verbal/Linguistic	Audioboo; QuickVoice	Become DJs and summarize events in a reading selection or characters through talk-radio conversation
Verbal/Linguistic	Pages	Write a news story in which you summarize what happened in a particular chapter or create a character biography or obituary
Visual/Spatial; Musical/Rhythmic	iMovie, Camera Roll, Animoto	Create a movie version of a short story, chapter, or scene, or create a music video analyzing a character
Musical/Rhythmic	Songify, AutoRap	Write a song about a character or reading selection
Verbal/Linguistic	Weebly	Create a website over a text or characters in a text
Verbal/Linguistic	Twitter	Create tweets that summarize chapters from a text; tweet as if you are the character from a text
Interpersonal	News Booth, Intro Designer Lite, iMovie, Camera Roll	Create a news report covering important events from a text or analyzing characters' actions
Intrapersonal	Blogger, Evernote	Write a blog as if you are a character; keep track of class notes by blogging; create a blog that summarizes chapters from a text
Visual/Spatial	Puppet Pals, Sock Puppets	Recreate a scene from the text to appeal to a younger age group
Logical/Mathematical	Timeline Builder	Create a timeline of events for a reading selection
Verbal/Linguistic	Evernote	Write a diary as a character; summarize chapters for each reading selection
Visual/Spatial; Verbal/Linguistic	Keynote	Create a presentation analyzing a character to present to the class
Visual/Spatial	Glogster; Pages; Keynote	View virtual posters people have created about texts; create a poster summarizing a text
Verbal/Linguistic	Gabit	Speak as if you are a character from a text, analyzing that character's perspective, what has happened to him or her, and POV
Interpersonal	Keynote	Have students present a presentation to review certain chapters of a text to review for a final test
Interpersonal	Explain Everything, ShowMe, ScreenChomp	Create video to teach other students about a reading selection; create a video teaching about a character's traits and motivations
Visual/Spatial	Kabaam	Summarize events in comic form
Verbal/Linguistic; Visual/Spatial	iMovie Trailers	Summarize a reading selection as a movie trailer
Interpersonal	Padlet, Neat Chat, TodaysMeet	Have students discuss a reading selection in a chat room

TABLE 9.2 Student choice board

Create a collage using the Pic Collage app	Create an iMovie project	Create a Keynote presentation
Create a comic using Kabaam	Create a Book Trailer using iMovie	Write and record a song with AutoRap
Create a timeline of events with Timeline Builder	Create a flyer using Pages	Create a picture book with Storybird
Create a video with ShowMe	Create a blog entry as a character with Blogger or Evernote	Organize the important information/events into a Popplet or Sticky Notes file

However, if we are reading a novel, and a student wants to listen to it, I will give them two options. First, if the book is free, I will ask for it to be downloaded onto their iPad via iBooks. All iBooks have the option for reading aloud; students simply need to highlight the page and select the "speak" option, as long as the speak selection option is turned on in the Settings of the iPad.

If I can't find an iBook version of the book, I will then try to find a chapter or two on YouTube. I have been able to find videos of people reading classics on YouTube. I have found selections for *The Scarlet Letter, Huck Finn*, and much more. I will usually copy the link and post it to my Schoology courses for students to access. On days in which I give students a chance to read in class, students simply need to click on the link, plug in their headphones into the iPad, and listen along.

While I give students the opportunity to listen to reading selections, I usually inform them that on most standardized tests, they will not have this privilege. Thus, as the year progresses and we get closer to testing time, I will usually not post YouTube links and encourage students not to use the speak selection feature on the iPad. This is to ensure that students are reading on their own and truly preparing for a testing environment.

Advanced Organizers with Tools 4 Students

Another type of app that I have not used much, but other teachers in my school have had luck with in the classroom is the use of organizers. Tools 4 Students is an app that can appeal to visual/spatial learners that need to organize information that they read. The app comes with different templates that students can use and e-mail to teachers. The app comes with templates for understanding cause/effect, identifying character traits, compare/contrast, pro/con, drawing conclusions, fact/opinion, KWL charts, making predictions, problem/solution, the plot curve, timelines, and more (Figures 9.1–9.3). Thus, the app can be used for both reading instruction and organizing/pre-writing purposes as well.

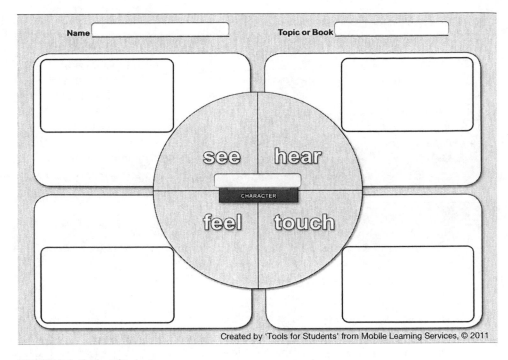

FIGURE 9.1 Tools 4 Students

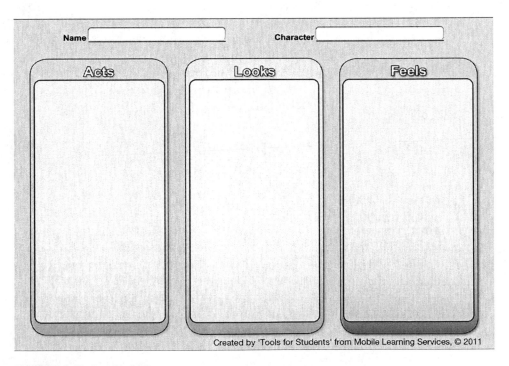

FIGURE 9.2 Tools 4 Students

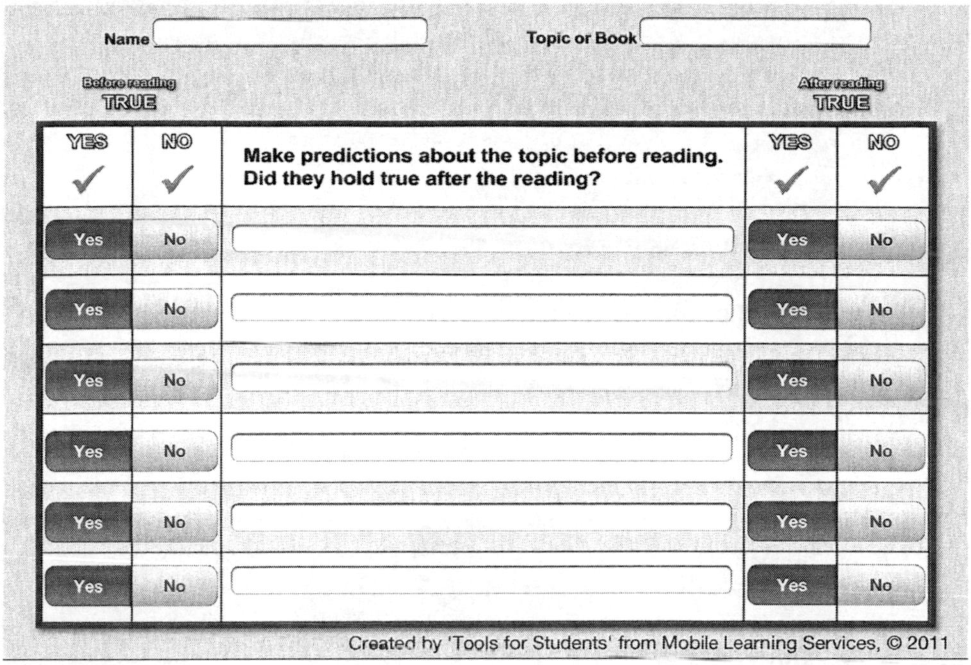

Before reading TRUE		Make predictions about the topic before reading. Did they hold true after the reading?	After reading TRUE	
YES ✓	**NO** ✓		**YES** ✓	**NO** ✓
Yes	No		Yes	No
Yes	No		Yes	No
Yes	No		Yes	No
Yes	No		Yes	No
Yes	No		Yes	No
Yes	No		Yes	No

Name [ ]   Topic or Book [ ]

Created by 'Tools for Students' from Mobile Learning Services, © 2011

FIGURE 9.3 Tools 4 Students

Technology-based Accommodations

Throughout the course of two years with the iPad, I have noticed that there is a new area of differentiation that all teachers using technology must be aware of. With technology, we not only must differentiate to ensure that students learn core content, but I have found that I also need to be aware of the fact that each student has his or her own background with technology. Students, especially in a district as economically diverse as mine, have different experiences with technology. In any given class period, I have students who walk into my classroom who are ready to use some of the more complex apps while there are others who do not know where to locate the power button. This is something that needs to be addressed to ensure that all students are not only being challenged, but challenged at the appropriate level.

When I first received my iPad, I originally thought that all students would be able to teach me how to use it. While many students were comfortable from the minute they opened it up, I have encountered quite a few students who have absolutely no experience with the device.

Thus, one of the biggest adjustments that I have had to make in the classroom this year is the fact that some (not many, but enough that it needs to be addressed) absolutely struggle to understand and use the iPad. I have had students enter the classroom not able to type well on the iPad and loathe the use of some of the complex apps. Thus, with technology's presence in the classroom, it is important to understand students' struggles with the device, how to intervene, and account for an app's complexity when creating lessons.

I've encountered students who struggle to efficiently type on the iPad. As a result, these students tend to despise essay-writing; while they also struggle to type on a regular keyboard, I have noticed that these students tend to type on the keyboard by pecking at it with their fingers. More outspoken students tend to complain about how slow they type on the device.

There are a few ways for students to type more efficiently on the iPad. First, Verbally is an app that I have suggested students use and have downloaded on the iPad for students to type essays.

The app is easy to use. Students type in words and as they type specific words, the app will give suggestions to finish the word. Thus, students only need to type in a few letters of a word, it then appears, and students only need to tap the word instead of typing it all. Figure 9.4 shows how students can use the app.

I find that the app is best suited for days in which we are typing for a lengthy amount of time, such as typing essays. With the app, students can type using the app, and then copy their words into a word-processing app or paste it into an e-mail to themselves to then paste into a word-processing app at home.

The only problem my students have encountered with the app is that they must proofread. As you can see in Figure 9.4, the app will not capitalize names or provide punctuation when a user taps on a generated word. Students must proofread and add punctuation in themselves. All in all, the app does work if you have a student who struggles to find letters on the keyboard. Just keep in mind that even after they type text, they must proofread.

If you have a student who works better through talking, Dragon Dictation is an app that will allow a user to speak into the iPad's microphone. Once a user

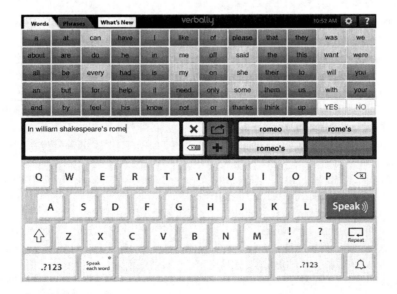

FIGURE 9.4 Verbally

speaks into the iPad using the app, the spoken words will appear as text. I have recommended this app to students who work better by vocalizing their thoughts or struggle to type on the iPad's keyboard.

However, few students use this app in my classroom. The primary reason why is because in a classroom environment, the app does not work well. A user must clearly speak into the iPad, and quite frankly, the iPad can pick up other noise. As a result, the text will, at times, not match what the user has said. Moreover, I have found that some students hesitate to speak into the iPad as everyone else is quietly typing. I am sure some do not use it because they do not want to feel embarrassed. Thus, this is an app that may work better in a 1:1 environment, as students can record their text in the privacy of their home and then paste it into a word document. As with Verbally, students will need to proofread after they have recorded their text. Dragon Dictation, unlike Verbally, will put in punctuation if the user speaks it. For example, if I say "comma" in the app, an actual comma will appear.

Another way to help students type on the iPad is through splitting the keyboard. This helps a wide variety of students, not just the students who struggle with typing. Many students, regardless of ability level or experience with technology, are used to texting on their phones. Thus, they find that they type quickly when using their thumbs.

To help them, I will tell them that they can split the iPad's keyboard by tapping and holding the bottom right icon on the iPad's keyboard. From there, the keyboard will split, and the user can then type by holding onto the iPad and using his or her thumbs to type. Students who are used to texting find that this is a useful and efficient way to type essays.

A final intervention I have used with my students involves complex apps. I have found that some apps and activities with the iPad, such as iMovie and Timeline Builder, are more complex than others. Thus, this is important to keep in mind when planning lessons and activities.

I learned this the hard way when it comes to iMovie. I originally thought that students would be able to use the app to create videos right from the get-go. However, I learned quickly that just like me, students need to be taught how to use certain apps. If your students are using a complex app for the first time, Apple TV is a great resource to use to model how to use apps. In my classroom, my Apple TV is connected to my projector so that I can mirror my iPad through the projector. As a result, I can project my iPad to show students how to use complex apps before they use them on their own.

I find that this strategy works best with not only complex apps, but simple apps as well. It takes about five minutes of class time to walk students through an app that I want them to use. This helps a lot; it also helps deflect numerous potential questions, as students will already have had a tutorial on how to use the app. Thus, their focus and time can be spent on using the app to demonstrate their knowledge of the standard I want them to master and not on the technology. While Apple TV can be expensive, it is worth the money as it can save a lot of precious class time.

Conclusion

All in all, by differentiating with the iPad, students have been more engaged in course content. I have noticed that when students arrive to class early and wait for the bell to ring, they tend to flock to apps and websites that appeal to their individual interests. Thus, I find that by simply observing the apps students use before class begins helps me to stay on top of individual students and their specific interests. From there, I can keep that in mind when I create future lessons.

Moreover, with the implementation of technology in the classroom for students to use, we must be aware of the fact that students come from different backgrounds; just like they all have different abilities in reading and writing, they also have different abilities with technology. Thus, modeling how to use technology and crafting lessons/groups with regard to app complexity is definitely something to keep in mind when lesson-planning.

Looking Forward

As a result of our grant team's success with the iPads, our school board has made the decision to make our high school a 1:1 environment. This is something that our entire district is not taking lightly; we have dedicated the school year prior to going 1:1 preparing all teachers how to use iPads in their classrooms. Each teacher in the high school has his or her own iPad to use and has had a year to experiment with it. We have extra iPad carts for teachers to check out. We have developed an iPad committee to address potential issues in a 1:1 environment. We have dedicated staff meetings to sharing best practices and apps. We are generating a list of essential paid apps for students to have on their iPads (when buying in bulk, some apps are half price). We are truly trying to ensure that each teacher is ready for all students having their own iPad. This is crucial to success; the iPad means nothing if it is not being used to enhance instruction and teach core standards.

While this process is definitely exciting, there is a lot of trepidation among our staff, myself included. With my own iPad cart, I have been responsible for charging my own iPads. When each student has his or her own, policies will have to be put in place for when students forget their iPads or do not charge them. I have a feeling this will be the biggest issue, as other schools have had this issue. When this occurs, I will undoubtedly have a discipline system and have students complete the task at home for a reduced grade.

From a teaching standpoint, the biggest change I anticipate will be the issues that arise from the fact that students are responsible for their own iPad all day long, and I can no longer control how many iPads are in my classroom each day or their battery charge.

One other change I am excited about is the fact that I can assign many of the assignments highlighted in this book for homework. With a class set of iPads, my students have been restricted to completing assignments in class. Now that they will be able to take their own iPads home, I can have them complete many of these tasks outside of class and teach more content.

Despite all of the work to transform my classroom, I know that I still have a lot of work ahead of me. There will always be new apps and tools available in the immediate future that will continue to bring a new dynamic to my classroom. This transition to a classroom centered on student usage of technology has opened my eyes to the next steps. The tools highlighted in this book are just the tip of the iceberg.

Through these conversations on the iPad committee, professional development, conversations with colleagues, and discussions with Apple itself, there are many resources that I personally have been ready to implement with my students for quite some time. However, I personally believe that these tools I am about to outline are more appropriate for a 1:1 environment. These are tools, ideas, and programs that can only further enhance and transform the classroom environment.

Creating a Paperless Classroom

From the minute I learned that iPads would enter my classroom, I immediately thought I would become a paperless teacher. My days fighting the copier were finally over, and I would finally be able to kiss the copier goodbye once and for all.

When it did not occur my first year, as I simply was not ready for it and did not have the knowledge base to do so, I thought it would happen my second year with iPads, especially as I implemented Schoology. I failed to become paperless my second year as well. There are a couple of reasons why.

To put it bluntly, becoming a paperless teacher is a task that will arguably take years. Making copies is something that has been engrained in almost every teacher; to suddenly not make copies of handouts is truly something that takes time. It is something of which I always need to be cognizant to make such a change.

More importantly, after conversations with teachers, parents, and students, I found that to have a paperless classroom would put those students without Internet at home at a disadvantage. Many parents told me that during a particular sport season, their child will complete homework on the bus on the way to a game. Thus, it worked better if they had an actual copy of the assignment and did not need to upload it or e-mail it to me. Furthermore, many students do not have study halls during the school day to visit our library to use the Internet; thus, some students can't access files or assignments at home and do not have the time to access them at school. I could not, in good conscience, become paperless and sleep at night knowing that I was placing stress on students to obtain course assignments. My goal is to create rigorous courses; obtaining class documents should not be part of this rigor.

Thus, I found that to try to become paperless when students do not have an iPad to take home would put some students at a severe disadvantage. The point of the technology is to enrich the classroom experience, not place more stress on students. Therefore, it is my philosophy that a paperless classroom is appropriate when all students can have access to course files. The only way in which this can happen is when they can complete it at home. Thus, a 1:1 environment, not a class set of iPads, is the best environment for a paperless classroom.

Based on my experience with the iPads, I do have a plan to become paperless in a 1:1 environment. The following are what I find to be the essentials to having a paperless classroom.

Schoology or Some Other Social Networking Site

Social networking is essential to implementing and maintaining a paperless classroom in a 1:1 environment with iPads. You will need to create assignments, create discussions, and upload files/handouts/rubrics for your students to see. Furthermore, students will need to view files, upload videos and pictures, and take tests. Between both its website and app versions, Schoology is a reliable source to do all of this and so much more in your classroom. Even more, with Schoology, you can create tests for students to take in a paperless manner. With everything that it can do, Schoology is essential to not only creating, but also maintaining a paperless classroom. If students need to upload a file, they can do so when they connect to the Wi-Fi in our school's building. If students need to download a file to view at home but do not have Internet, they can do so before they leave the school building. All in all, it's an essential resource, especially as you transform your classroom and students create videos, photos, and other types of products.

E-mail

There are certain apps that do not allow files to be downloaded to the iPad's Camera Roll, and thus, can't be uploaded to Schoology. To view and grade these files, your students will have to share these with you in another method. Many apps without Camera Roll functionality will allow the user to e-mail. Thus, students will have to have an e-mail account to e-mail these files to you. Between the ability to upload to Schoology, or e-mail, students should be able to share virtually any file they create with you in some manner to view, assess, and grade.

Worksheets

As much as I try to replace worksheets in my classroom with apps or other tools, the worksheet does hold value for some assignments. If you want your students to complete a worksheet and e-mail it to you, Type on PDF is a great app for students to download a file, annotate it, and then e-mail it to you to grade.

The key with this app is that the file is a PDF file. Thus, I have sifted through all of my worksheets and saved them again as PDF files. This way, I can post the assignment on Schoology, students can download it, and from there, they can complete it. If you post a Microsoft Word file on Schoology, users will only be able to view the file on the iPad; they will not be able to write on it with a marker or type on it. Students without Internet at home can download the file during the school day, open it up in the appropriate app, and complete it at home, as it will already be downloaded on the iPad.

Word-processing App or Tool

For writing essays or formal papers, students will need to have access to a word-processing program. Many people prefer Google Docs, which is similar to Microsoft Word. However, my main problem with Google Docs is that it is not user-friendly on the iPad. I tend to favor the Pages app. It is one program in which students without an Internet connection can use at home. If they type a paper at home, they can send it to you at school via an Internet connection. Or, the day an essay is due, you can simply ask students to e-mail it to you at the beginning of class. Best of all, they can send it as a Pages, PDF, or Word file. Moreover, if students send me the file in a PDF format, I can annotate the paper with my comments with the Type on PDF app and send it back to them. After two years of using iPads and fumbling through different word-processing apps, Pages has come to be my favorite word-processing app.

Note-taking App

With an iPad, students will need a place to keep track of their notes. Students can take notes using the Notes function, one of the iPad's default features. However, this is not exactly the best tool to use to organize tabs.

With research, there are many note-taking apps available on the iPad. A few that look promising are GoodNotes and N+OTES. A popular one that many students and teachers like is Evernote. One that looks especially promising is mySchoolNotebook. This app, as opposed to others, seems as if it is especially tailored to note-taking in schools. The app separates a bookshelf into each school year. Thus, students can keep track of all of their notes from freshman year to senior year, and even beyond. From there, students can add notebooks with the name of the course and the teacher. From there, users can take notes. Users can also add audio and take a photo or video. Thus, this app can be used if students want to record a lecture, take a snapshot of what is being projected, and type notes on their own.

What seems like the best feature is the ability to make notebooks public and to share notebooks. Thus, absent students can get notes from a friend, or as an instructor, I can share notes with students. That way, students can listen to my lessons for understanding as opposed to focusing on writing down all content. Between all of the features in the app, this is one that I will use in my classroom in a 1:1 environment.

Between Schoology, e-mail, and a PDF annotation app, becoming a paperless teacher in a 1:1 environment will still take time, but at least it will be feasible. The importance of all these tools is that all students should have the ability to download a file before they leave the school building to complete it without an Internet connection, and upload it in some manner the next day at school when they have Internet.

Flipped/Blended Learning

Another area I wanted to tackle with the iPads is flipping the classroom. Flipping the classroom entails students watching videos of lectures at home; that way, class time can be spent by completing activities that will help students develop a deeper understanding of content, as classes will be activity- or project-based.

One of the greatest benefits of flipped or blended learning is that the teacher can move around the room to help individual students as they complete assignments, as they are spending less time teaching the class as a whole. This can lead to a deeper understanding of class material for all students, as the teacher can give more one-on-one time with each student.

I spent a great deal of time during the summer creating instructional videos covering different Common Core Standards and other important concepts that students could watch at home. Figures 10.1 and 10.2 show exactly what these videos look like. Students first watch the video at home. Then, the next day,

FIGURE 10.1 Flipped videos

FIGURE 10.2 Flipped videos

we would briefly discuss the concept in class, and as a result, my classroom would become based around activities. In short, students would learn concepts at home through instructional videos, and we would spend class time completing activities based around what they already learned in the video.

My plan at the beginning of the year was simple: I uploaded the videos to my Schoology course pages. Students would watch the videos as they related Common Core Standards by accessing them from our Schoology course (Figure 10.3). Class time would then revolve around activities for students to show deep understanding of these concepts.

However, I encountered the same problem that I found with being a paperless teacher. I could not, in good conscience, assign these videos for students to watch for homework knowing that many of my students could not watch them, as they did not have Internet access at home. Therefore, I ditched the flipped model for the time being; I posted the videos on Schoology for students to watch on their own time if they did not understand a concept. I would not assign, but rather encourage students to watch these videos for homework, as assigning it for homework would put some students at a severe disadvantage.

Creating these videos took time, and without a doubt, the most important thing to keep in mind before creating them is to have a place for students to view these videos. I find that Schoology allows users to easily upload videos with the iPad from the app. You can also upload videos to schoology.com as long as you are on a laptop or PC.

When preparing to film, I spend time outlining the standards and concepts I want students to master and create a video for each one. I created separate videos about summarizing, paraphrasing, MLA formatting, writing a thesis, demonstrating using textual evidence, themes, conflicts, foreshadowing, writing

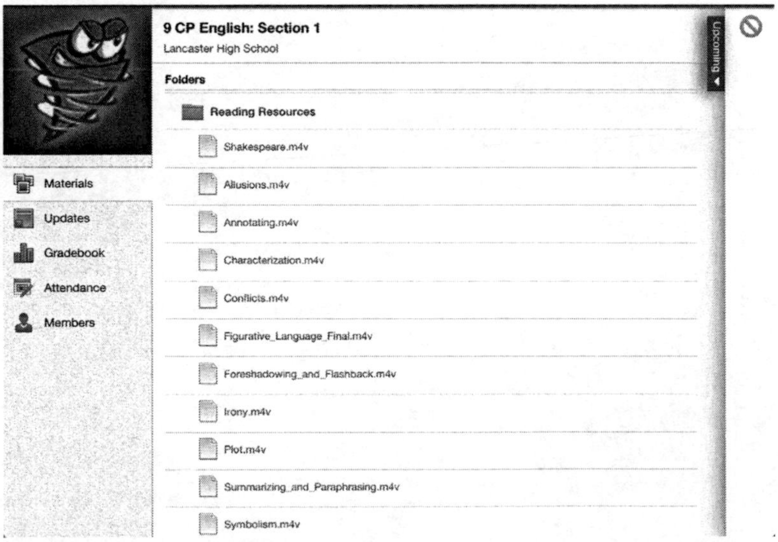

FIGURE 10.3 Schoology flipped video folder

TABLE 10.1 ELA standards/ideas for flipped videos

Allusions	Persuasive Techniques
Annotating a Text	Figurative Language
Grammar Concepts	Foreshadowing and Flashback
Characterization	Irony
Writing Essays (one video to discuss each paragraph)	MLA Formatting and Citations
Conflicts	Writing a Paragraph
Defining Words using Context Clues	Plagiarism
Shakespeare Conventions	Reliable Internet Sources
Symbolism	Themes
Summarizing versus Paraphrasing	Writing a Thesis
Transitions in Writing	Identifying Tone and Mood
Parts of the Plot Curve	Crafting a Works Cited Page

dialogue, narratives, persuasive essays, and so much more. Table 10.1 provides a list of different concepts for which English teachers can create their own videos. For each video, I bullet the main aspects I want to discuss on a piece of paper, and then record the video, making sure I addressed those bulleted points. Each video is about three to five minutes in length, enough to discuss the concept at hand, but not so long that it becomes unbearably boring to watch.

There are three main ways in which you can create your own instructional videos, whether you want to implement the flipped model or just want students to have a resource to review concepts. First, if you have an iPad, you can open up the camera and record videos. From there, it will save to your Camera Roll for you to upload to a website. This is, without a doubt, the easiest way to create a video for flipped instruction.

For iPad users who want a more sophisticated-looking video, you can open the iMovie app and add text, music, titles, and sound effects to your video clips. All you have to do is add your video clips to a project by either filming within the app or the iPad's camera. From there, double-tap on the selected images to add titles, click the music icon to add music or sound effects, and click the photo icon to add photos.

Due to the fact that my school has provided me with a MacBook, I prefer to use iMovie on my MacBook. This is what I typically use to create these videos, as the Mac version of iMovie can create movies that look truly professional. The Mac version has some sophisticated features, such as green-screen capability, picture-in-picture, and split-screen effects. I have a light green cloth that I have used in the past as a bulletin board. With iMovie on the MacBook, I was able to use this as a green screen to change the background for different videos. Many YouTube video searches helped me find information on how to do this. All you need to do is type in "create movie in iMovie app" or "iMovie on Mac" to learn how to do so.

Finally, there are videos in which I wanted to record my desktop computer screen and narrate during this recording. The website screenr.com is a great tool to use to record your desktop or laptop screen for up to five minutes in length. For videos over MLA formatting, I went to Screenr, set up an account, and then positioned the part of my screen I wanted to record. From there, I recorded myself setting up a paper in MLA format in Microsoft Word, explaining exactly how to do so. I have created similar videos on how to integrate quotes and how to write a business letter. The only thing you need to have to use Screenr is a microphone and a PC/laptop.

Between the iPad's Camera Roll, the iMovie app, the Mac version of iMovie, and Screenr, there are many tools available to create instructional videos if you want to implement flipped/blended learning in your classroom. The most exciting aspect of implementing these videos in a 1:1 classroom is that students can watch the video at home. From there, we can spend a few minutes at the beginning of class discussing the concept. From there, most of the class can be spent completing assignments and activities; I can walk around and help individual students instead of lecturing most of the period. This will help students obtain a deeper understanding of all of these concepts. All in all, these tools allow anyone to create videos that create a new facet to teaching and learning.

Transforming the Textbook

One of the most eye-opening professional development experiences I have ever had is when Apple came in to talk about iBooks Author with our grant team. iBooks Author is an app on MacBooks and iMacs in which a user can create an interactive iBook that users can then open up on an iPad.

When I first went to the PD on iBooks Author, I will admit, I was skeptical. I believed that our textbooks were fine the way they were; after all, it is an online textbook that works perfectly on the iPad. However, as the speakers discussed the different features available to users of iBooks Author, I began to realize exactly how they can create a brand new dynamic to reading literature in an ELA classroom.

This is because iBooks Author has quite a few valuable features that can make reading a completely new and interactive experience for students. These features are known as widgets. Once I have imported different reading selections in my textbook, I can create widgets on each page to help students further understand the specific reading selections. Widgets that can be created and/or imported include:

- Keynote presentations;
- video/audio files;
- review questions;
- pictures;
- hyperlinks;
- 3D images; and
- so much more!

Creating an iBook with iBooks Author

Creating a book is easier than the iBooks Author program looks. The way in which I create one is simple. I first open up the program on a Mac and then select a template. From there, I create a title page and then begin copying and pasting my reading selections that I have found from Google searches. From there, I create my different widgets. To create these widgets, I find PowerPoints, worksheets, instructional videos, and comprehension questions.

With all these widgets in mind, creating a book can be a daunting task. When I first started creating a textbook using iBooks Author, I had trouble deciding exactly how to organize it. After trial and error and experimenting, I quickly decided that the best way to organize an iBook textbook would be to create one for each quarter of the school year. This is to keep the file sizes for each book as small as possible.

I'll give you an example. With my freshmen, we devote the first nine weeks to studying the theme of "judgments." We first read short stories connecting to this idea, then we read *To Kill a Mockingbird*, and finally, students write a narrative over a prompt about a time in which they were unfairly judged.

The way in which I organize the iBook is exactly how I organize this first nine weeks. I first begin with a cover to the book, a table of contents, a page that gives an overview of the unit, another page for the quarter's learning targets, copies of the reading selections, and narrative-writing resources. Since *To Kill a Mockingbird* is not considered public domain and copying it into an iBook would break copyright laws, I do not put the book in my textbook. From there, I create widgets to help students learn different literary concepts as they read each selection. These typically relate to a pacing guide I follow throughout the school year.

If the widgets work the way they are used when I test my copy of the book, it will create a brand new experience in reading for my students. I can pose questions for students to answer. Students can discover different widgets by clicking on different pictures and videos. The use of widgets will reinforce concepts taught in class. It will help with flipping instruction, as instructional videos will be available in the iBook. iBooks Author allows teachers to create textbooks and truly tailor them to how they teach each piece of literature. This can help ensure no stone is left unturned and that students obtain an enduring understanding *over all literary concepts* on a regular, consistent basis. Students can also annotate pages with Post-it notes, use the dictionary to define words, have the iPad read passages aloud, and so much more. These are all features that can both stimulate successful readers in new and innovative ways and also help struggling readers understand how to become better readers, as I can create widgets that give hints at important concepts to analyze on each page of a text.

I will admit that creating a book is extremely time-consuming. Finding the reading selections is not difficult; most of the novels and selections that I teach are easily found on the Web. However, the different widgets take a lot of time to make. I have found that, by taking the worksheets, comprehension questions, and different resources I have already accumulated throughout my career saves time, as all I have to do is type them into my iBook. Moreover, due to the fact that Keynote can transfer PowerPoint files, I have also imported PowerPoint files I already have by saving them to my Mac as Keynote files.

Even still, creating an iBook takes time. The best piece of advice I can give is to work with your fellow grade-level teachers to create different iBooks that you can eventually share with one another. This is extremely beneficial, especially if you work with people who teach the same texts and follow the same pacing guide as you. I work well with my fellow freshman teachers, and we each teach the same texts. Thus, we have divided the work among the three of us. I am responsible for creating an iBook for the first nine weeks, another is responsible for the second, and another is responsible for the third nine weeks. Once we have completed them, we will put our books on a USB drive to share with one another. Since we will each have our own copies of one another's files, we can then open up the books in iBooks Author and individualize them to how we teach each work. This will definitely save time and a lot of unnecessary work.

The most exciting aspect of creating an iBook for students is the fact that I will never again have to worry that our school has enough copies of a text. I, and I am sure other teachers have fallen victim to this as well, have found myself in the predicament in which I wanted to teach a novel, but due to the fact that other teachers were teaching it at the same time or poor planning on my part, there were not enough copies available for my students. As a result, I either would have to scramble to change my plans, try to find used copies of the book, or ask students to find a copy of a book. With iBooks Author and a 1:1 environment, I will not have to worry about this unless the book is not in the public domain.

Even though I have created my own iBooks textbooks for my classroom, I have decided not to introduce them to my students until my school goes 1:1. The reason why I put these on hold is due to the fact that, with all of the videos, Keynote presentations, questions, and other features, an iBooks textbook is best geared primarily toward independent reading. With only a class set of iPads, students could not watch the videos in class, as it would be distracting for other students around them. Moreover, with most of my classes, I assign most of the reading to be completed outside of class. Thus, while I have completed iBooks for my classroom, it is a feature best implemented when students can access it on their own iPads and use at their own leisure. When this occurs, I will share my iBooks I have made with my students via e-mail.

Siri and Reminders

With an update of its iOS operating system, Apple's newest generation of iPads now have the ability to activate Siri. Siri will perform many tasks. When you tap and hold the "home" button on the iPad, you can tell Siri to find directions, find apps, go to particular websites, and so much more.

I have used these features on my iPad. Siri is a great way to create reminders. With so many tasks to remember, I always used to write reminders throughout each day on Post-its. By the end of a given school day, I would have so many Post-its stuck to my desk calendar that I would quickly become overwhelmed. With the iPad, I have eliminated these Post-its by using Siri and/or the Reminders function. With Siri, I can create a reminder by simply tapping the home button and speaking into the iPad. That way, if students need me during one of my free periods, I can stay in my classroom to make sure they can find me, as my iPad will alert me at the appropriate time.

When my school goes 1:1, I am going to encourage students to use Siri, the Reminders feature and the Calendar to keep track of homework and different due dates. In addition, for those students who have trouble turning in work, I will encourage them to use Siri or the Reminders feature. For any student who frequently does not turn in work, we are going to come up with a plan for them to get reminders when they get home to do their homework. This way, they will have someone other than me hounding them to get work done. If work is still not completed, this is an intervention I can inform parents about when I call them on the phone or during parent-teacher conferences.

Moreover, Siri is a tool that all of my students can use. If we have a due date that is far away, I will tell students to create reminders a week before that assignment is due. This way, students will not forget about it and will still have ample time to complete it unless, of course, they decide to procrastinate.

Places to Find New Tools and Apps

The tools available to iPad users will constantly evolve and change; as a result, as I look forward to more years with mobile devices, I will continue to search for apps, tools, and activities in my classroom. In the beginning of implementing iPads, this became extremely time-consuming. There are so many websites available to search for tools to use that it could take months to view them all. Teachers do not have time to go through all of these resources.

That is why I have limited my daily searches for apps down to one main website. One website in particular, scoop.it, provides a collection of different blogs geared toward technology and iPads in the classroom. Many of these blogs are regularly updated; as new apps are available, they are highlighted in new posts. In fact, the scoop.it website has a whole collection of blogs dedicated to technology. Blogs such as iPads in Education Daily, Learning Technology, and more have introduced me to so many apps that I have used with my students. While these websites do not always explain how teachers of different content areas use particular apps, the scoop.it website is a great resource to find constantly updated information and new apps or tools to use with your students.

Also, I can't stress enough the importance of networking with other teachers. Schoology has teacher groups, such as 1:1 Computing, Language Arts, and more, dedicated to helping one another troubleshoot technology issues, ask questions, and share tools. Edmodo, a social networking website similar to Schoology, has teacher groups as well. The English Companion Ning is another website to collaborate with other educators and find discussion threads about technology in the ELA classroom. While there are so many more resources of using iPads in the classroom on the Web, these are the most reliable for new tools, ideas, management strategies, troubleshooting, and more.

Collaboration with Other Teachers and Schools

Schoology, Edmodo, and the English Companion Ning are great places to not only network with other educators, but I have tried to collaborate with others via these websites as well. As more schools look forward to a 1:1 environment, these are places to find someone to Skype or FaceTime together, share writing samples, and so much more.

If you want to try collaborating with other teachers around the world, I would start with any of these three places. However, keep in mind that the logistics of finding someone to collaborate with via Skype is extremely difficult. When it comes to implementing Skype in the classroom, I would first try with someone within your school building; a great way to begin is to find someone with the same class/prep in the same period. From there, work out a lesson or discussion that you can have together with both classes. Most importantly, test-call one another a day before you begin the lesson to ensure that it will work.

Conclusion

All in all, when I am able to look back on this time with technology, I feel as if I have grown more in this time than ever before. The apps and tools highlighted are only the beginning of this journey; there is so much more available that I know that my classroom will continue to transform as I become introduced to more tools and more apps are developed.

As technology evolves and a 1:1 environment becomes the norm in American education, I can't help but wonder how beneficial it would be if teachers had more of a hand in the development of apps/programs for their own classrooms. For every app I have found, I can think of five more that could directly influence my instruction and that of other English teachers as well. As we become experts with technology in our classrooms, we are the ones who will eventually know what apps and tools we would want to see. There are computer programs (X Code, for example) available to create apps, but the coding involved is time-consuming and way beyond the expertise of many educators, myself included.

Without a doubt, the most rewarding aspect of this technology is observing my students using it. They are interacting, collaborating, and creating products in ways I never thought possible in the classroom. The true change in my instruction has been the way in which students demonstrate their knowledge, as they have done so primarily through authentic assessments. With the iPad, students have done much more than read and write in the classroom. In the course of a year, they have become:

- readers;
- writers;
- authors of picture books;
- songwriters;
- talk show hosts;
- music video editors;
- advertisers;
- cartoon creators;
- website creators;
- poets;
- historians;
- filmmakers;
- comic creators;
- radio show hosts;
- news anchors;
- teachers;
- bloggers; and
- so much more.

They have completed all of these tasks on the iPad, all the while learning the reading and writing skills to prepare them for college and their future careers. My hope is that at least one of these tasks on the iPad has ignited a passion in them that will eventually lead to a future career direction.

Even if this does not occur, the student engagement in my classroom is unlike past years. This is due to the fact that students are creating products that they take pride in and assignments are holding more relevance than ever before. While not every activity or lesson ran smoothly or perfectly, the iPad has created an environment in which students are learning and having fun. As Apple's App Store further expands and more tools become available on the Internet, the opportunities for more creativity and engagement in the classroom will only expand. As excited as the technology has made me about teaching, I can only believe that it has made students more excited and engaged as well.

Appendix: Rubrics and Assignments

Weebly.com Website Assignment Rubric (___/100 Total)

Website Appearance	Points possible	My points
Website is attractive and easy to navigate.	5	
The webmaster has clearly spent time making the website look professional.	5	
The website has photos and/or videos to make navigation truly interactive.	5	

Introduction		
The home page has an effective attention-grabber.	5	
The home page gives an overview of the topic of the website.	5	
The introduction gradually leads into a thesis statement.	5	
The introduction has an effective thesis statement.	5	

Body		
The body paragraphs have effective topic sentences and transitions.	5	
The writer has seamlessly blended outside research with the ideas presented in body paragraph 1.	5	
The writer has seamlessly blended outside research with the ideas presented in body paragraph 2.	5	
The writer has seamlessly blended outside research with the ideas presented in body paragraph 3.	5	
Each body paragraph feels as if its topic sentence has been proven.	5	

Conclusion		
The conclusion wraps up the paper by recapping the main points.	5	
The writer gives a final analysis and point to give the paper closure.	5	

Grammar and Spelling		
The writer has proofread for spelling and grammar mistakes.	10	

MLA Formatting		
The writer has correctly cited sources in MLA format.	10	
The writer has correctly formatted and written a Works Cited page.	10	

A Story Before Bed Story Narration Assignment

Now that we have discussed the qualities of effective narration, you and a partner are to create an account in the A Story Before Bed app. From there, pick one of the stories and practice reading the selection as if you were reading it to a young child. Once you feel you have an effective narration, e-mail the video to me through the app. You will be graded with the following rubric:

Area	3	2	1	0
Pitch	The speaker varies his or her pitch throughout the entire selection to engage the audience throughout the entire video.	The speaker varies his or her pitch, but can be a bit monotonous at times.	The speaker rarely varies his or her pitch to engage the audience.	There is no attempt to vary the pitch.
Rate	The speaker varies his or her rate and understands how punctuation affects the reading of a text.	The speaker varies his or her rate, but could do more with it to create suspense and emotion.	The speaker barely varies the rate or speed of reading.	There is no attempt to vary the rate.
Volume	The speaker can be heard and volume differs to match what happens in the selection.	The speaker varies volume, but he or she can vary it a bit more to engage an audience.	The speaker is heard, but is a bit soft-spoken at times.	The speaker can barely be heard.

Animoto Introduction

To become better acquainted with one another, we are all going to create a video montage of ourselves with the Animoto app. For this assignment, you will need to bring in photos. You can either e-mail pictures of yourself or you can bring them in. From there, we will use the Animoto app to create these videos. We will then watch them by uploading them to our Schoology course page.

The idea is to get to know one another better. Thus, you should highlight different aspects about yourself. Topics you can include:

1. Favorite movie, book, activity, etc.
2. Sports you enjoy.
3. Goals.
4. Where you are from.
5. Any interesting tidbits about yourself.
6. Other hobbies or items of interest.
7. Anything else that you want us to know!

Character Popplet Assignment

DIRECTIONS: Create a popplet in which you take the different characters, monsters, and gods from *The Odyssey* and describe them based on how they act or what they say. Each of your popplets must have the following:

- The name of the character.
- What the character says or does (make sure you have direct textual evidence with a citation).
- What the quote reveals about the character.

You must have five popplets completed. E-mail them to me when you are finished by taking a screenshot of the entire popplet and e-mailing it to me through the iPad's Camera Roll.

Here is how I will grade you:

_/5 The writer *correctly* uses direct textual evidence for each popplet.

_/5 The student responds to the quote with an analysis of the quote and what it reveals about each of the five characters.

_/10 Total

CHARACTER WORD CLOUD ASSIGNMENT

Your assignment is to create a word cloud. This word cloud is to be about a main character from the text. To create one, you first need to come up with 10 words that relate to your character. Post them below:

_____   _____
_____   _____
_____   _____
_____   _____
_____   _____

Now that you have your words, you can create your word cloud. Your word cloud can be created with the following tools:

Word Foto   Wordle.net   Tagxedo.com

Make sure more important traits are more prominent in your cloud. You can do this by typing important words numerous times. When finished, save your photo and upload it to our Schoology course. You will be graded on whether or not your words highlight important character traits.

The Crucible Radio Show:
Act I

With a partner, develop a talk radio show in which you discuss the important aspects in Act I of *The Crucible*. Use the Audioboo app to record up to three minutes. Add radio sounds from YouTube and other apps to make your product sound like an actual radio show! You must address the following:

___Rev. Parris

___Tituba

___Abigail

___Betty

___Susanna Walcott

___The Putnams

___ The Nurses

___Mary Warren

___Mercy Lewis

___John Proctor

___Rev. Hale

You will receive one point for mentioning each character.

The Crucible Radio Show:
Act I

With a partner, develop a talk radio show in which you discuss the important aspects in Act I of *The Crucible*. Use the Audioboo app to record up to three minutes. Add radio sounds from YouTube and other apps to make your product sound like an actual radio show! You must address the following:

___Rev. Parris

___Tituba

___Abigail

___Betty

___Susanna Walcott

___The Putnams

___ The Nurses

___Mary Warren

___Mercy Lewis

___John Proctor

___Rev. Hale

You will receive one point for mentioning each character.

The Crucible Radio Show:
Act I

With a partner, develop a talk radio show in which you discuss the important aspects of Act I of *The Crucible*. Use the Audioboo app to record up to three minutes. Add radio sounds from YouTube and other apps to make your product sound like an actual radio show! You must address the following:

___Rev. Parris

___Tituba

___Abigail

___Betty

___Susanna Walcott

___The Putnams

___ The Nurses

___Mary Warren

___Mercy Lewis

___John Proctor

___Rev. Hale

You will receive one point for mentioning each character.

iMovie Infomercial Assignment

Now that you understand the basics of a process speech and an infomercial, in a group of three, you will create an infomercial or an HGTV segment demonstrating how to use a product you have created. It should illustrate your understanding of not only giving clear instructions, but understanding of what happens to vocal quality when you are demonstrating how to do something. I will grade your group on the following:

Content Scores	4 points	3 points	2 points	1 point	0
I have a script/outline that clearly plans out the video.					
I have an introduction that grabs audience attention and introduces the product.					
I clearly explain how to use my product with step-by-step instructions.					
I have a conclusion with a memorable line.					
My infomercial clearly illustrates awareness to its intended audience.					
Delivery Scores	4 points	3 points	2 points	1 point	0
I have vocal inflections that are appropriate to an infomercial.					
All group members use appropriate volume.					
I use gestures/expressions appropriate to an infomercial.					
My eye contact makes the audience feel involved.					

Figurative Language Assignment

Become an Expert

Now that we have reviewed the different types of figurative language, you will show your knowledge of it by creating a lesson over a particular type. Using a whiteboard app, you will create a lesson that explores everything about your assigned type of figurative language. In your video, you should address:

_/2 I have a definition of the type of figurative language and a way to remember this definition.

_/2 I have two sophisticated examples (do not Google; come up with these on your own).

_/2 I have two overused examples that should be avoided.

_/2 I have two examples from literary works we have read this year.

_/2 My video is creative and interesting to watch.

__/10 Total

iMovie Character Music Video

To understand character traits and why certain characters act the way they do, you are to create a music video with music, text, and pictures that describe one of the characters. You will use the iMovie app to create this video. In this music video, you are to do the following:

_/2 Describe the way the character behaves. What do his or her actions tell you?

_/2 Describe the character's motivations. How does he or she act? What does he or she want?

_/2 Describe the way the character looks. What image comes to your mind? (Find pictures and import them into your project.)

_/2 Who or what does the character like or dislike?

_/2 What is the overall importance of this character? Why is he or she in the text?

_/2 Textual evidence (integrate and cite in MLA).

__/12 Total

Please export your file to the Camera Roll and upload to our Schoology course for others to view and for me to grade.

iMovie Commercial Assignment

Your final assignment with persuasion is to create a commercial that illustrates correct use of different persuasive techniques. You must create a commercial geared toward a specific audience/group of people. You can pick your demographic. From there, you will create an advertisement in iMovie to get that group of people to buy a specific product. Your commercial should include the following:

Area	3 (Superior)	2 (Proficient)	1 (Below Standard)	0 (No Attempt)
Appeal to Emotion				
Appeal to Reason				
Appeal to Authority				
Rhetorical Question				
Call to Action				
Correct use of parallelism				
Audience Awareness				
Authenticity of Commercial				
Creativity of Commercial				
Correct Spelling/Grammar				
Total __/30 points				

IMOVIE SUMMARY MUSIC VIDEO

Using your collages that you created for each chapter of the text as a guide, you are to create a review video that summarizes the important events of *Of Mice and Men*. You must address all of the main points in sequential order. You should add music, text, and pictures to illustrate your knowledge of the text. This will help you as you review for your upcoming final test. You will be graded on the following:

___/3 Main points of Chapter 1 are addressed

___/3 Main points of Chapter 2 are addressed

___/3 Main points of Chapter 3 are addressed

___/3 Main points of Chapter 4 are addressed

___/3 Main points of Chapter 5 are addressed

___/3 Main points of Chapter 6 are addressed

___/2 Overall product (music, pictures, and text) reflects the tone and mood of the text

_____/20 TOTAL

INDEPENDENT READING PROJECT

Assignment: This nine weeks, you are going to select a novel, read it, and then create a radio show in which you discuss the novel. Here are the following guidelines:

1. It must be at least 150 pages.
2. It must be appropriate to your reading level and interests.
3. It must be school appropriate.
4. It CAN'T be a novel you have already read.

You will find and bring your book in on Friday. I will then look at it and approve it.

This is a two-part project worth 52 points! Do not wait until the last minute to read!

PART ONE: SCHOOLOGY DISCUSSION POSTINGS
(20 POINTS)

You will log in to Schoology and reply to four discussion postings about your book. You will also respond to at least two other classmates' responses. Here are the deadlines for the postings:

Posting #1: due by September 30
Posting #2: due by October 7
Posting #3: due by October 14
Posting #4: due by October 21

PART TWO: RADIO SHOW
(32 POINTS)

Then, the last week of the quarter, you will be creating a radio show informing us about your book. In your show, you will give a summary of the novel, examples of direct and indirect characterization, overview of the setting, themes/morals, archetypes, and other literary terms.

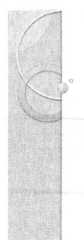

INDEPENDENT READING PROJECT: PART 2

Now that you are finished with your novel, you are to create a radio show informing your classmates about it. You are to script out a radio show and record it in class with the Audioboo app. Once you are finished, you will upload the link to your radio show to Schoology. You should address the following:

Area	4	3	2	1	0
The radio show host provides an attention grabber and introduction to the show.					
The radio show host provides a summary of the novel.					
The radio show host explains different archetypes.					
The radio show host explains examples of direct/indirect characterization.					
The radio show host explains themes in the novel.					
The radio show host explains conflicts and classifies them.					
The radio show flows and transitions are used throughout.					
The radio show provides an effective conclusion.					

Love Letters to Penelope with Evernote

DIRECTIONS: After you have read each of the encounters from Part I of Homer's *The Odyssey*, write a letter to Penelope in the voice of Odysseus that demonstrates not only your knowledge of the encounter, but Odysseus's desire to return to her. In each letter, you must have:

■ A summary of the encounter.

■ A description of the god/goddess introduced in the encounter.

■ Odysseus's reaction to the events.

You must have a letter for each of the encounters in Part I. When you finish your letters, share your notebook with me through the Evernote app.

You will receive three points *per letter.*

OF MICE AND MEN IMOVIE TRAILER ASSIGNMENT

oNow that we have finished reading *Of Mice and Men*, you will create a trailer to show your knowledge of the text.   You should address the following in your iMovie Trailer:

A basic summary of the text
Music and trailer template that matches the mood of the piece
A theme statement
A logical trailer that looks professional

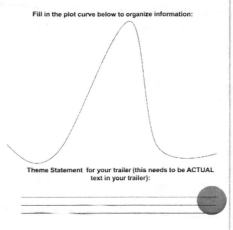

Fill in the plot curve below to organize information:

Criteria	3	2	1	0
A theme statement is in the trailer				
Trailer summarizes the entire text				
Trailer's music and background match the overall mood of the piece				
Trailer is planned by filling out story's the plot curve and theme statement to the right				
Coherence of video				

Theme Statement for your trailer (this needs to be ACTUAL text in your trailer):

To Kill a Mockingbird Character Scrapbook Page

Now that we have read a few chapters of *To Kill a Mockingbird*, you are to create a scrapbook about one of the characters using the Pic Collage app. In this collage, you are to *directly* address:

_/2 Collage has pictures of the character (look for evidence from the text and find pictures that relate to what the text explicitly states).

_/2 Collage has words/phrases that explain the character's personality.

_/2 Collage addresses who/what the character likes and dislikes.

_/2 Collage has a sentence explaining the character's motivations.

_/2 Collage has at least one piece of textual evidence (integrate and cite in MLA).

__/10 Total

Romeo and Juliet Puppet Pals
Talk Show

In your group of three, create a talk show video in which you show your knowledge of your assigned act from the play. You should have an AUTHENTIC talk show that addresses the following...

____/5 Summary of the act through conversation

____/3 Character Conflicts in the act (don't forget to classify them!)

____/5 Character motivations are explained

____/2 Video looks and feels like an actual talk show

BE CREATIVE! YOU CAN PRESENT THIS INFORMATION IN A CREATIVE MANNER; JUST MAKE SURE YOU PRESENT THE INFORMATION IN THE RUBRIC!

Scene Study Assignment

Now that we have read two acts of *Romeo and Juliet*, it is time for you to show your expertise of a particular scene. Using either Animoto or iMovie, create a video in which you analyze a specific scene.

In your video, you must address...

_____/4 What occurs in the scene

_____/2 A conflict from the scene (classify)

_____/1 One Shakespearean convention in the scene (an actual quote)

_____/3 Quality of the product

_____/10 TOTAL

Schoology Informational Text Discussion Threads

During the first quarter of the school year, you will be given an article to read outside of class each week. Your job is to read the article and then post a reaction to it in our Schoology course discussion threads. After others have reacted to it, respond to them by asking questions, making connections, and bringing up new ideas.

By the end of each week, you should:

- Post an initial reaction to the article.
- Respond to others in the class throughout the week; have an actual dialogue/debate/conversation with others. Have fun with this! Don't be afraid to disagree with one another!
- Cite the article at least once as you discuss it with other students throughout the week.

I will grade your responses with the following rubric:

_/3 The student posts an initial reaction to the article on Schoology by both *reacting to it and emphasizing the main points of the article*.

_/3 The student *provides evidence from the text*; it is integrated/cited correctly and helps prove the student's point.

_/3 The student has stimulated discussion throughout the week by *respectfully responding to at least three other students*.

_/9 Total

★★Your responses are time-stamped in Schoology; therefore, make sure you post your responses on time!★★

★★If everybody waits until the end of the week to post an initial response, it will be difficult to stimulate the discussion *throughout the week*!★★

"Song of Myself" Romantic Poem

Now that we have read Walt Whitman's "Song of Myself," you are to write a poem about yourself. The poem must contain the following:

-3 stanzas, 5 lines each
-Information about yourself
-An insightful connection between you and nature
-Poem must relflect the qualities of a Romantic poem
-Use of figurative language

After you have written your poem, you will use the TellaStory app to record your poem. You will then add nature noises and a nature image to your poem. E-mail these to me by the end of class.

Songify Figurative Language Song

- Your assignment is to create a song with different types of figurative language. You are to define and give an example of the following types of figurative language. Once you have your definitions and examples, open up the Songify app to create a catchy and memorable song to help you to remember these different figures of speech. Fill out this planning sheet to help you with your song:

- Simile:_____
  - Ex:
- Metaphor:_____
  - Ex:
- Personification:_____
  - Ex:
- Alliteration:_____
  - Ex:
- Hyperbole:_____
  - Ex:
- Imagery:_____
  - Ex:
- Oxymoron:_____
  - Ex:
- Onomatopoeia:_____
  - Ex:

Speech Critique: Part One

In at least *one page*, write a critique explaining the strengths and weaknesses of the speech you just gave. Make sure you evaluate the following:

- Content: introduction, body, conclusion, and signposts.
- Delivery: eye contact, gestures, vocals, and body language.
- Audience interest and interaction.

To receive full credit, you must address all criteria and also *specifically* explain what was strong and weak. You should also suggest ideas as to how to improve for your next speech.

Speech Critique: Part Two

From there, you will then create a video in which you explain the strengths and weaknesses highlighted in your critique in a one- to two-minute video. In this video critique, you should focus on the following:

- Speaking with an engaging pitch, rate, and volume.
- Using effective gestures.
- Using appropriate facial expressions.
- Using appropriate eye contact (look at the iPad's camera).

Think about your written critique and try to work on your weaknesses as you provide a narration of your strengths and weaknesses as a public speaker!

Overall, this is a 15-point grade. When finished, you can upload your videos to our Schoology course.

Storytelling Vocal Quality Practice Assignment

DIRECTIONS: Using your iPad, open up the Puppet Pals app. Using your manuscript and annotations, create an entertaining puppet show that showcases the vocal quality you may have during your actual storytelling speech. You should practice the following:

- Using a lively and effective narration.
- Varying your pitch to entertain your audience.
- Speaking with a faster rate as your story builds to a climax.
- Using distinctive character voices.

Once finished, export your videos to the Camera Roll and post them to Schoology using the app. Once you have done so, watch others' videos and give them feedback on how to improve their vocal quality.

The Salem Times

You and a partner are writing for the local Salem newspaper. Act as if you witnessed the court proceedings and now need to summarize the events in Act III of the play for the rest of the town. Using the Pages app, find an appropriate template and create an AUTHENTIC newspaper in which you...

____/4 Summarize events from Act III of *The Crucible*

____/2 Summarize characters' fates (Who is sentenced? What will their fates be?)

____/2 Give predictions of what will happen in Act IV

____/2 Create a product that looks and is designed as an actual newspaper page (you may need to research some newspapers with a Google Images search)

Tweet Away!

While we read *Romeo and Juliet*, you will be responsible for picking a main character and providing periodic tweets in the voice of that character. Your tweets should reflect what the character knows, finds out, and/or what happens to him/her. From there, you should also provide the character's reaction to that event.

We will use these tweets to review aspects of the play.

Why did Rosaline have to take the vow a chastity? I know! I'll go to the Capulet ball and find her!!

Romeo

Romeo, why are you a Montague!! Does a name really mean anything anyways?

Juliet

The Ultimate Guide Newscast

- Now that we have finished reading our short stories, you will create a resource video to show your knowledge of an assigned short story. In your group of three, you should address the following....

Direct/indirect characterization examples
Examples of conflicts and classifications
Figurative language examples
The plot curve
Character descriptions
Round/flat/static/dynamic characters
How the text relates to our quarterly theme

There are different apps you can use to create a newscast. They include:
iMovie
IntroDesigner
NewsBooth

Criteria	3	2	1	0
Understanding of direct/indirect characterization				
Understanding of conflicts				
Understanding of figurative language				
Story's plot diagram				
Character Descriptions				
R/F/S/D Characters				
Themes explained				
How this relates to our quarterly theme				
Creativity of video				
Coherence of video				

Website Video Analysis with Explain A Website

Now that we have discussed what makes a website reliable, you are to create a video in which you evaluate whether or not a website is reliable. You must first find a reliable source and explain its validity based on the following questions (write notes down about your website on this sheet so that you know what to say).

Author:

- Who is the author?
- If there is not an author, what is the name of the institution or organization running the website?
- Why is this person/organization an expert in this area/topic?

Bias and thoroughness:

- Does the website present information without favoring one side?
- How thorough is the website? Roughly how many facts do you think you will be able to take from this source?

Timeliness:

- Has the information been updated recently? When?

Purpose of the website:

- What does the author or organization want from its visitors?
- Does the website try to get you to buy something or have advertisements?

Sources used within the website:

- Does the author cite other reliable sources?

Export your video to the iPad's Camera Roll and upload it to our Schoology course by the end of class!

List of Tools

Tool	Use/Lesson
SplashTop (app) Weebly (website)	Users can control their projected desktop or laptop with an iPad Students can create and publish a website in place of a research paper
Schoology (app and website)	Gives the ability to implement social networking in the classroom; a place to upload attachments, videos, create discussions, tests, and much more
Type on PDF (app)	Gives users the ability to annotate a PDF document; save worksheets as a PDF and send to students; students can then fill in the answers with the app, and e-mail them back to you
Kabaam (app)	Comic creator; students can create a comic to summarize/ storyboard what they have just read
Storybird (website)	Picture book creator; students can type their narratives with the website to produce a professional-quality picture book
Toontastic (app)	Cartoon creator; students can create a cartoon of narratives they have written or ask students to pre-write their narratives with the app
CloudOn (app)	Students can type essays with the app; must have a Dropbox or other cloud-based account
Dropbox (app and website)	Students can create a digital portfolio and access files both on Dropbox app and website
Pages (app)	Students can write essays, and create resumes, business letters, flyers, newspapers, and so much more with this word-processing app; many templates to choose from
Skitch (app)	Teachers can annotate essays to show students how to format or write essays correctly. Users can annotate pictures and other files with the app
Explain a Website (app)	When reviewing reliable versus unreliable sources, students can find a source to explain in a video why it is or is not reliable to use for a research paper

Flashcardlet (app)	Students can create flashcards for vocabulary quizzes; students can use the app to organize research for a research paper
T-Charts (pro and con) (app)	Students can pre-write for a persuasive or argumentative essay with this app
iMovie (app)	Students can create commercials, character videos, summaries, and so much more with this movie-making app; students can create summary and thematic trailers with the Trailer option
iTellaStory (app)	Students can write nature-inspired poems and record them with this app; great app for making poetry audio-based and come to life
Songify and AutoRap (apps)	Students can create songs out of poems; great for regurgitating class notes to a beat or style of music
Gabit (app)	Students can create 30-second videos in the voice of a character explaining his or her motivations and actions; great for recording poems about characters
Animoto (app and website)	Students can create a music video about themselves, a character, or summarizing a short story
Evernote (app and website)	Students can create journals that can sync directly to your own Evernote account, a great way to obtain students' journals in a paperless manner; students can create character diaries or letters in the voice of a character
Poll Everywhere (website)	Great for agree/disagree anticipation guides; formatively assess the whole class over a specific concept through the use of polls
iBooks (app)	Students can read and annotate books on the iPad; many classics are available to download for free in Apple's bookstore
Createqrcode. appspot.com (website)	Teachers can create QR codes to websites to make visiting websites easier as a class
RedLaser (app)	Students can scan projected QR codes to visit a website
Keynote (app)	Students and teachers can create presentations or slides; similar to PowerPoint
Puppet Pals (app)	Students can create puppet shows explaining a text
Intro Designer Lite (app)	Students can create text introductions for a movie; great when used in conjunction with iMovie
News Booth (app)	Students can create pictures for a newscast; great when used in conjunction with iMovie
Popplet Lite (app)	Students can create mind maps to pre-write for an essay; students can create mind maps to show knowledge of concepts
Tagxedo.com (website); Wordle.net (website); WordFoto (app)	Students can create word clouds about a character or a word cloud summary of a reading selection

Timeline Builder (app)	Students can create a timeline of events for a reading selection; students can add titles, descriptions, and pictures
Pic Collage (app)	Students can create a collage of a character, or summarizing events from a text
Explain Everything (app)	Teachers can create flipped instruction videos; students can create figurative language videos; great tool for teaching and recording lessons; one of the few reliable whiteboard apps that saves videos to the iPad's Camera Roll
Screen Chomp, Show Me (apps)	Whiteboard app, great for review games; Show Me has an archive of lessons and tutorials from other users
Shakespeare in Bits (app)	Show cartoons of scenes from Shakespeare plays; full text versions of Shakespeare plays; many other great features; great for projecting onto a whiteboard
Ye Olde English Insults (app)	Shakespearean insult generator; students can insult one another and try to find meanings
iPoe, iPoe 2 (apps)	Students or class can read interactive versions of Poe short stories, a great way to make Poe's short stories come to life
Socrative (app and website)	You will need both the student and teacher app; teachers can create quizzes, exit slips, space race review games, and other formative assessments to see whether or not students understand a lesson with teacher app; students take quizzes with the student app
Sticky Notes (app)	Students can create a board of sticky notes to show what they know or review for a final test
Schoology tests (available on app or website)	With a Schoology account, teachers can create tests that students can then take on the iPad; results can be automatically transferred to a Schoology grade book
Jeopardylabs.com (website)	Teachers can create *Jeopardy* templates that can keep track of scores; thousands of pre-made templates that users can surf through
Neat Chat (website)	Students can communicate in groups, teachers can hold thesis workshops, and students can discuss a text in this chat room
Padlet (website)	Students can discuss a text via pictures, text, and video in this visually stimulating website
TodaysMeet (website)	Students can communicate and collaborate or share ideas up to 140 characters at time; great way to force students to be concise in writing
Twitter (website and app)	Students can tweet in the voice of a character with this app or website
AnswerGarden.ch (website)	Ask students questions and the most popular responses will show up as the largest text; great way to see which concepts the class as a whole wants to review

Camera Roll (app)	Students can record video diaries, diaries in the voice of a character, and re-enact key scenes from a reading selection
A Story Before Bed (app and website)	Students can record a video of themselves as they read a children's book; great way for students to practice vocal quality in preparation for a storytelling speech
Skype, FaceTime (apps)	Absent students can Skype in to ensure they do not miss important speeches or presentations; great tool to use to collaborate with other classes or schools
QuickVoice (app)	Students can record themselves to practice vocal quality before they give a speech
Tools 4 Students (app)	Students can access and type in numerous graphic organizers; great for pre-writing, summarizing, ordering events, analyzing characterization, and so much more
Verbally (app)	Great tool for struggling typists; students type and the app will generate recommended words to tap on to complete the word; helps struggling typists type faster
Webnotes (app)	Students can take notes from the Web; great for research or annotating from an online textbook
Audioboo (app)	Students can create podcasts or radio shows to discuss their knowledge of a text
Dragon Dictation (app)	Students can speak into the iPad's microphone and text will appear; great for struggling typists as long as they are in a quiet environment
iBooks Author (app for MacBook)	Create course textbooks and send them to students' iPads in the form of an iBook; import texts considered public domain and import widgets to create an interactive reading experience
myschoolnotebook, N+OTES, Evernote (apps)	Students can keep notes in one specific place on the iPad; myschoolnotebook will organize students' notes based on class and school year; great way to keep a record of notes in a 1:1 environment
Siri (activated by tapping and holding the iPad's "Home" button)	Create messages/reminders; great for students to remind themselves of important assignments; great for remembering important teacher-related tasks

References

Common Core Standards. © Copyright 2010 National Governors Association Center for Best Practices and Council of Chief State School Officers. All rights reserved.

Gardner, H. (2011). *The Unschooled Mind: How Children Think and How Schools Should Teach*. New York: Basic Books.

Koehler, M.J. (2012). What is TPACK? Retrieved from http://tpack.org/.

Partnership for 21st Century Skills (2011). A Framework for 21st Century Learning. Retrieved from www.p21.org.

Tomlinson, C.A. (1999). *The Differentiated Classroom: Responding to the Needs of All Learners*. Alexandria, VA: ASCD.

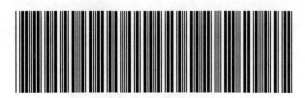